totidem verbis ... semel insanivimus omnes!

(in just so many words ... we have all, at some time, been mad!)

Collected Poems and Stories

by

Adam Donaldson Powell

Collected Poems and Stories
_by_
Adam Donaldson Powell

Cyberwit.net
4/2 B, L.I.G.
Govindpur Colony,
Allahabad-211004 (U.P.)
India
Tel: 91-532-09415091004
E-mail: cyberwit@rediffmail.com
www.cyberwit.net

Cover : The day after – New York City, Ground Zero
Painting by Adam Donaldson Powell

ISBN 81-8253-028-8
First Edition: 2005
Rs. 150/-

Typeset by Vaishnavi Enterprises, Kamla Nagar, Allahabad
Printed in India at Astha Associates, D. N. Marg, Allahabad

DEDICATION

Dedicated to the memory of Tor Vågli (1949 – 2004)
and the countless Asian tsunami victims of 2004.

CONTENTS

POETRY CYCLE 3

POETRY CYCLE 4

HORROR

POETRY CYCLE 1.

The Magical Tarot through verse

The Fool

The cautioning crunch of air compressed between
Boot and dust-ladened pebbles goes unheard as
Aleph the Fool steps naively onto the pavement.
Overhead, the spirit of ether condenses into
Illusory nimbus formations which shield his
Half-opened eyes from the apparition of Zelotziel.
He is neither a true believer nor cynic, but rather
An empty vessel longing to be replenished with
Seductive impressions of colorful indiscretion.
I recognize in his fixed smile the arhythmic
And pained beating of my own lonely heart: a
Reminder that nothing risked is nothing gained.
Sadly, the quest of the Fool lacks awareness
That Truth's magical portrait will be unveiled
Only after the snarled process is complete ..
And that the Tarot's mysterious paintbrushes
Are inherently dualistic.

The Magus

Seemingly employing nothing more than
Air, water, fire and earth, the
Magician adeptly balances yin with yang
In swirling spheres of Mercurial energy.
His power to renew lay not in the
Uncovering of mysteries, but in the
Tempering of reason with understanding.
Truly, the angel Raphael appeals to all
Who are enchanted by magic or change:
'dare to strive .. dare to succeed.'

The High Priestess

The Priestess of the Silver Star
Meditates upon the horn-shaped moon
With open eyes, and attunes her heart
To Gabriel's mystical song of knowledge.
Her spiritual earnestness joyously
Melts the shackles restraining the
Collective unconsciousness' reserves of
Reflection, which then drizzle from
The starry sky like zillions of
Particles of mirrored-confetti.
This magnificent cloudburst of astral
Light illuminates an auric crown of
Beauty about the mistress of the tides,
And intuition yields understanding.

The Empress

Internal rumblings emanating from the
Womb's darkness signal the workings
Of the archetypal Great Mother.
Her deep-rooted secrets define the
Wonders of fertility and multiplication,
Which culminate in fulfillment of
Creative instinct and maternity.
Many are her names: Gaia, Rhea,
Juno, Isis and Pasiphae.
Truly, the powers of the daughter
Of the mighty ones go unchallenged
In the world of science and men,
And will forever remain a symbol
For the art of unselfish loving.

The Emperor

As the weary morning sun climbs the
Rugged, red-gold horizon of Mars,
The Chief of the Mighty Ones
Peppers ambitious sand drifts with
Wisdom of soverignty and beauty.
A sudden flash of desert lightning,
Illuminating the severe image of the
Ancient ram-god Horus, is fate's
Reminder that growth and stability
Are provided on the condition of
Loyalty to the authority which binds.

The Hierophant

The gentle, warm winds of Vau
Whistle softly through cypress-
Forested valleys obscuring the
Sixteenth Path of the seeker.
Obscurity caused by earthly illusion
Is penetrated by rays of pure light
Issuing forth from the merciful staff
Of the prudent Shepherd of Souls.
To those thirsty enough to hear,
His unspoken counsel to preserve and
Endure is imbibed solely from the
Ever-filled cup of continuance.
Right action is to be taken at
The appropriate moment, and the
Grace of the present holds the
Treasures of the future.

The Lovers

While the allure of the secret garden
Lay in the promise of Paradise regained,
The strange fruits hanging from its
Lowest boughs yield but bittersweet
Marriage of affection and need.
Knowing that no entity is complete in
Itself, the Children of the Voice Divine
Adjust their own shortcomings and
Graces after the responses of those
They interact with.
Together, their diverse personalities
Conspire to reach the more distant but
Sweeter fruits of harmony, and in that
Unity find divine love and realization
In an otherwise imperfect world.

The Chariot

The Angel of Cancer protects industry
And advancement from the powers of Evil
By tempering severity with understanding.
At his disposal are thirteen vigilant
Full moons, and a fanatical charioteer
Called the Lord of the Triumph of Light.
Initiated souls distract not this driven
Chauffeur with small talk, for he too is
A passenger of the enigmatic sphinxes.
Nay, no one rests easy on this whirlwind
Carousel; guaranteed arrival is little
Consolation for the bewildered in transit.

Adjustment

Over the heads of the righteous
Hovers the pendulous blade of
The Daughter of the Flaming Sword,
Magically balancing beauty and
Soverignty with severe Truth.
Those blinded by self-confidence
Mercilessly plummet into temptation's
Shameful abyss, whereupon adjustment
Is sentenced and administered by
The impartial Lords of Karma.

The Hermit

Many a fool and solitary hero
Would dismiss the rantings of
The hermit, who acclaims the
Virtues of discretion and reserve.
But even angels fear to sleep amid
The entourage of a leader who has
Lost his way, and where all is not
Necessarily as one would suppose.

Fortune

No amount of glitter and glamour
Or sleight of hand on the part of
The Lord of the Forces of Life
Can outshine the passionate will
To succeed in the true believer.
Zealous onlookers egg our player
Of the Wheel of Fortune on to higher
Stakes, where both celebrity and
Russian roulette await those who
Would test the flow of destiny.

Lust for Life

Those who lust for life
Recognize that challenges
Are a means to victory,
And that linkage with
One's archetype gives
Persistence needed to
Attain self-realization:
That most beautiful
Jewel of them all.

The Hanged Man

For those who would save
The world for personal
Gain, the hanged man's noose
Is but a romantic vice.
But he who sublimates
Himself to the Divine Plan
Recycles the elements to the
Accompaniment of Spirit.

Death

Forbidding visions of moon-parched
Skulls with infra-red light glowing
From vulture-ravaged eye-sockets warn
The curious and the soul-dead against
That which does not concern them,
For admittance to the ever sacred
Fields of Transmutation and Catharsis
Is by invitation only.
The well-oiled hinges on the gates of
Death never creak over human tragedy,
But rather rejoice at the prospect
Of purification and recirculation of
Mass and decomposing archetypes into
New forms of energy.
Tending this soil, so richly imbued
With essence of fertility, is an
Age-less, cloaked gardener who works
In silence and darkness; and who,
From time to time, shakes his head
In bewilderment over the futility
And masochistic madness of those who
Would resist transformation.

Art

Sun-dipped arrows propelled from the archer's bow
Rain upon clouds of illusion with great moderation,
Thus revealing a splendiferous prism of multi-colored
Light gracefully emerging on the horizon.
Sadly, the wisdom of action and consequence symbolized
By this beautiful phenomenon escapes both dreamer
And planner — who, for all their brain-activity,
Cannot see the forest for the trees.

The Devil

Beware.
The dark one
Lurks not in
The shadows,
And not amongst
Your friends
Or enemies.
Beware, for
His evil lies
Within you,
And eagerly
Awaits release
By descendents
Of Pandora.
Beware of
The road to
Inertia and ruin,
So carelessly
Littered with
Temptation and
Obsession.
Beware.
The self-centered
And worshippers
Of false splendor
Can expect
Little more than
Disappointment.
Yes. Beware
Of darkness ..
And beware
Of mirrors ..

But most of all
Beware
Of the devil
That you are.

The Blasted Tower

We're all match-stick architects,
Forever building precarious
Structures to contain and conceal
Our inhibitions and fears.
With disaster a constant risk,
It's little wonder we're
Paranoid and fearful of the
Flaming element of surprise.
But don't bother looking
Often over your shoulder
Or crossing your fingers.
And you may as well trade in
The garlic and crucifixes for
Worry beads because, in
Reality, each of us is
But a walking time-bomb.
By the way ..
Do you smell something
Burning upstairs?

The Star

From the still-warm ashes
Rises the phoenix toward
The star of Tzaddi; and
In the calm that follows
That clamor of mighty wings
Beating life into the ruined,
The soul and mind of Man is
Rejuvenated by hope and faith.

The Moon

Under the aspect of Pisces
The goddess of the Moon
Sheaths human perception
With delusory grandeur.
She appeals to dreamers
And masters of imagery,
Who would readily intuit
Without really seeing.
Her impressions serve as
Guidance and her promises
Are many, but he who mistakes
Vision for truth courts folly.

The Sun

Michael,
The angel of healing and
Lord of the Fire of the World,
Soothes broken Spirit with rays
Of divine light beamed from
The eternal flames of the sun
To the heart-centers of the
Children of Paradise.
This infusion of divine luster
And peace radiates inner joy
With auric resplendency,
Creating foundation for
Contentment and success.

The Aeon

The observers of the passage of time
And guardians of future challenges
Seek out and further those initiates
Of the Way who would use learning from
Past mistakes to promote evolutionary
Development by blending logic with
Understanding of human nature.
There, in the wake of spiritual rebirth,
The now-experienced Fool attunes himself
To the eternal vibrations of the Source,
Where he dances to the ageless tonalities of
The New Order, and exercises good judgment
In following the well-choreographed movement
Prescribed by the masters of the Zodiac.

The Universe

As True Will eclipses with the
Night of Time our ritual approaches
The completion of a spiritual cycle,
Where self-discipline and habit
Have yielded autonomy and fertility.
Enslaved by our new-found freedom,
We willingly endure the momentary
Darkness and await deliverance from
Our perfect womb to unknown challenges
In our next expression as the Fool.

Suit of Wands

From the gaseous, primal roots of
The flaming triangle is invoked
Energy of the Divine, that life-force
Giving rise to creativity and birth.
He who meditates upon this sacred
Source of strength and virility finds
Hasty solution to all inquiries.
But the restless heart that lacks
In concentration or enterprise
Fails to unravel the tightly-wound
Ball of thread veiling the lower
Mysteries, and its fervent endeavors
Are rather rewarded with barren
Pursuits and endless false beginnings.

Suit of Cups

In the blackness of Venusian
Subconscious and magic dangles
A luminescent crescent moon,
Kinetically poised in between
Undefined poles of space and time.
Hypnosis lures the lover toward
Lunar tides of joy and beauty,
Where on a sunken peak of rock
And moss awaits the Lady of Waters
Extending a silver chalice.
To him who would willingly fill
The sea-grail with his blood flows
The wine of splendor, and to the
Nonbeliever the empty cup reveals
Turbulence reflected in his soul.

Suit of Swords

Don't be fooled by appearances.
He who stands before you in
Readiness with poised sword,
Will strike if challenged.
By the severity of Saturn
And strength of Mercury,
He furthers advancement by
Wielding victory over strife.
Don't be fooled by appearances.
He is concerned neither with
Emotion or reason, but the sport
Of conquest through discipline.
Fear rather his mind and use of
The powers of air than his sword;
It is his mastery of these weapons
Which will determine the outcome.

Suit of Disks

Ruling over the world of
Physical manifestations
And material power is
Jupiter, Giver of Fortune
And Father of the Sky.
The wise journeyman reaps
The harvest of his toils
In accordance with his
Understanding of the laws
Of nature and action.
Those less inclined to heed
Celestial warnings gamble
With the elements and risk
Loss to the disastrous
Consequences of impatience.

POETRY CYCLE 2.

Selected short stories through verse

The Prudent Cognoscente

Strolling through the
Barrel-lined aisles
With her ladened cart,
The prudent cognoscente
Pauses periodically to
Admire alimentary delicacies
In open display.
She sneers at the spanish oranges,
Which are bruised and overripe;
And cringes at the inferior broccoli —
So yellow and dry.
But her eyes alight with
Discovery and glee as
She tosses aside the lid
Of the last garbage can
And silences the nonsensical
Cravings of her refined palate
With the simple charm of
Garden greens and aged brie.

Modern Times and the Old Negro

I remembers one hot 'n dusty mornin'
On the road to Realism:
Bus couldn' ha' been more 'n nine miles
Outside the Big City when the
Air-conditionin' gave out.
The upright, sunburn-wrinkled faces
'round me soon started a'meltin'
into sleepy country roads —
Like the ones ya sees on bank calendars:
With clapboard corner stores a'boastin'
Sales on 'Freudian Slips' an' plastic posies.
Yeah, ah jus' knowed ah be headed straight fo'
Hell, so's ah closed mah eyes real tight
Sayin' "Praised be the Lawd!"
Feelin' panicky that ah be most terribly lost,
Ah was jus' abouts to get off that bus,
When ah hears someone whisper "Niggar."
Well chil', ah gots mad fo' a minute,
But then ah jus' grinned like an
Old fly in a new outhouse 'cause
Suddenly ah knowed exactly where ah be.

The Adolescent Years

The adolescent years caught us off guard.
Fighting the travesties of acne and war
In a world we did not really know,
We marched through youth as soldiers of mercy
Compelled by the romanticism of mass dissent …
Feeling much, with little certainty.
If knowledge vanquished gullibility,
Then surely inexperience bred expectation;
And faith cradled us in naked dreams
Of prodigious sexual love yet bereft
Of both lust and rationality.
I remember how you once told me that
The sexiest word in the french language
Has to be "pamplemousse".
You broke up in laughter and exclaimed:
"It means grapefruit. Can you believe that?
G-R-A-P-E-F-R-U-I-T!"
I laughed because your amusement was contagious.
Looking at your wild eyes and farm-girl smile,
I fell captive to your callow charm and
Soon we were deep in each other's arms,
Giggling hysterically.
We awoke from our laughter gazing at
One another in momentary sobriety.
And then, I buried my head in your breasts
Whispering "p-a-m-p-l-e-m-o-u-s-s-e!"
And our seriousness died laughing.

Stud

Responding to the call
Of a warm summer night,
The muscled youth surveys the
Streets from his Oakland stoop
With the vigilance of a vulture.
He soothes the heat
Pervading his loins
With beer and cigarettes,
And gyrates to rhythms
From his sony walkman to
Intensify his baiting scent.
At the passing of each female,
He extends greetings and suggestion —
Lastly to a haughty one who
Requests that he kindly 'drop dead.'
The youth throws a kiss and laughs
In sport and self-defense,
Until he spies the adoring stare
Of another boy, and yells:
"What are you looking at, faggot?!!"

Private Moments: Homage to Chicago

October winds lick at my shirt-tails
Like a cat eating ice cream;
But the cold only encourages my oblivion,
For it is emptiness that I seek.
Dead to the sirens rushing corpses
To their moment of truth,
And limp to the prey of wayward housewives
Shivering on shadowy streets,
I desire only to be alone with my private moments
Until the romance of despair numbs
My failed ambitions and consumes my pride.
And like all truly self-sufficient men,
I once again return home … alone …
To celebrate the birth
Of Winter.

AIDS .. Also a Vampire's Lament

In the Spring of our rapture,
You assuaged my hunger
With gallant love-bites and
Wept rubescent teardrops
As my own offering
Cascaded willingly into the
Vessel of your thirst.
Thereafter,
Enchanting midnight promenades,
Serenaded by love-sick werewolves,
Inevitably climaxed with
Splendiferous candlelit repasts
Of aristocratic blood plasma
And the finest port wines.
Magically abducted by the ecstasy
Of transfusion and reminiscence,
We who are forever young
Renewed our vows of
Never-ending devotion with
All the certainty and bliss
Intrinsic to incipient passion.
So golden were our halcyon days —
Yet unblemished by the ravages
Of overfamiliarity and diseased blood,
Now yielding insomnious forenoons
In separate coffins and
Solitary meals under would-be
Romantic moonlight.
Since our greatest promise
Has become your heaviest burden,
I look upon eternity as
The merciless side-effect
Of myopic infatuation …
And dream, perhaps,
Of growing old.

The Death of Poetry

Fifteen years ago —
When poetry was still popular —
My creative writing teacher preached that,
While history repeats itself by nature,
A good poet never does.
Frowning particularly upon
'that ever-stuttering Gertrude Stein'
and assailing the Beats as opportunists
in an age of trend, he warned
that the death of poetry
was approaching and that its demise
would precipitate intellectual senility.
The spunky old man lives in a rest home now,
And barely recognizes me when I visit.
Yet, nothing can tarnish the love I feel
As he excitedly engages me with the same
Damn stories I've heard for fifteen years,
Over .. and over .. again.

Writer's Blues

Seated in a quiet corner in his favorite restaurant,
The barren-minded writer waits patiently
For a seizure of etymological inspiration.
It's been days since he has eaten and
Perhaps longer since he has really slept,
For the agony of nonexpression is a
Leech upon his every desire.
Unmoved by the sophistication of the truckers,
Or the beauty of the waitresses and prostitutes;
And so untouched by the artistic vibrance
Of the orange and red interior,
The turquoise diner seats, and the
Choking Victim posters adorning the walls,
The writer assimilates in undisturbed silence —
Night after night —
Until even he no longer hears the
Occasional regular who leans close
To another, then points and says:
"You see that guy over there in the corner?
…. He's a writer!"

Je m'accuse

On the third of November,
As we danced in piles and flurries
Of autumnal foliage, and
Played hide-n-seek behind
Nameless statues and inmodest trees,
We transformed an acre of Central Park
Into the palatial gardens of Versailles.
Quietly within ourselves,
We both knew that our friendship
Was changing as the rotation of
The earth overtook the
Rhythms of our hearts,
Making us dizzy and childlike.
It seemed almost ludicrous that a
Taurean and a Piscean would
Endeavor to bridge land and sea.
And so, no sooner did you reach out
To touch my face than did I
Part my lips to speak
In distraction.
Then — captured by your stellar eyes
And crescent smile,
I arrested the first word in mid-breath
And surrendered my heart to sway
In the winds of confession:
"Je m'accuse … je suis amoureux."

The Dissident Android

From nine-to-five I am an android,
Programmed for industry and monotony.
I struggle to restrain myself against
Deviation during those hours,
Knowing that to live each moment
As if it were the first and the last
Would surely subvert the machinations
Of this music without silences.
Inevitably, as the noise of repetition
Soars to a deafening climax,
My tortured soul emits a
Violent scream of protestation
And breaks down in tears
Of mourning over ransomed
Moments of creativity.
It is not without desperation
That I await the sunset of sobriety,
When I can once again set pen to paper
And capture youth and illusion
In poetic refrain.

Drag Queen

You know — I hardly recognized you
Out-of-drag this afternoon!
Your clever disguise
Enabled you to sit down
Before I could run away.
You both surprised and intrigued me
When you lamented the slow
Passage of time — for I
Have often envied and despised
Your freedom and almost fickle
Sense of reality.
Funny how …
All these years …
I regarded you as crazy.
But now that we share disillusionment
With expectation and time,
I recognize you in myself.

Just because you're paranoid,

Doesn't mean you're not being followed!
(East Village, New York City — 1987)

As the crowd pushes me upward
From the darkness of the underground,
A mild panic begins to rush
Through my veins yielding
Torrents of sweat that race
Uncontrollably over my
Forehead and chest.
With just moments to spare,
I hasten to tear off my tie,
Roll up my shirt-sleeves, and
Complete my disguise with
The darkest of shades and
The meanest of scowls.
At the surface, my head begins to
Reel at the stench and sight of
Unwashed urchins and broad-smiling
Ne'er-do-wells with extended
Palms seeking tokens, cigarettes
And loose change.
My already shortened nerves are
Obliterated by the blasts of
Buick-sized radios carried by
Junkies and peddlars of items
Discarded by me the week before.
Looking about with hesitancy and
Anticipation — I shriek and recoil
In horror and disbelief:
The punks, thieves, beggars and
Schizoids are chasing me now!

…. Boom — Chiga-Boom,
Chiga-Boom-CHIga-BOOm-CHIGA BOOM!
Once home — saturated by disgust
And relief — I retire to the
Tv room with scotch and soda,
And eagerly await the news report
Concerning those who were
Not so lucky.

Scaramouche

On his deathbead,
My dear friend Scaramouche
Tried to convince me that
Life is a conundrum,
And therefore has no ending.
After pondering his hypothesis,
I thought to counter that
Conundrums are usually absurd …
But, of course,
I was too late.

Bridge Party

Certain that she will be
The toast of the bridge party,
The hostess gazes approvingly
At the mirrored reflection of
Her perfectly painted face,
Newly-coifed hair and stunning dress.
With the buzzer's announcement of
The first-arrived guests,
She eagerly starts toward the door,
Then pauses, and quickly
Sends the inquisitive child off
To play lest he betray all trust
And deflower the premiere by
Questioning the nature of the
Freshly-formed pimple on the
Tip of her nose.

While we wait ...

Patiently — we endure,
Desperate to believe in God, justice and humanity.
Repeatedly — we suffer
From our own ignorance and inmobility.
Admirably — we martyr ourselves,
Tranquilizing pain with saintliness and esteem.
Inevitably — we avenge,
Using the very tactics of our aggressors.
Ultimately — we are shunned
By all who thought we were extraordinary.
Typically — we wait
For the world to discover its misjudgment.
Ironically — we learn nothing,
And neither forgive nor forget.

L.A. Homeboy

Hey Homeboy!
Ran into Faith, your woman,
Up in the barrio last Saturday.
She wanted to know how her 'homeboy' is.
I told her you was still doin' time.
Her ma won't let her write,
But it ain't been the same, bro'.
Little Julio's started dealin' crack,
And she's two months pregnant.
When I asked her if the kid
Was yours, she started cryin'.
I didn't know what to do, man;
So I put my arm around her
And mumbled: "You gotta keep the fai…".
Then I stopped, dried her tears
And smiled, while sayin':
"If Homeboy was here, he'd tell you
to keep the baby, Faith."

Deja Vu

Last night,
While leafing through an old family album,
I saw an ancient photograph of my father
Modelling my Nehru jacket and hippy beads.
I smiled,
Remembering how he would always tell me
That one day I'd grow up to be 'just like Dad' …
It's strange to think that long hair,
Hitchhiking, and hit songs with singable lyrics
Felt no more ludicrous then than lavish
Christmases, gym memberships and nouvelle cuisine
Do now.
And I'm repeatedly amazed at how quickly
Personal revelations become 'period pieces' —
Modernity lasts but a mere second in
Life's journal of redundant cliches:
From white dress shirts to
Paisley to stripes
And back …
This morning,
While shaving in the bathroom mirror,
I frowned at my receding hairline
And then laughed to myself while
Thinking: you know — 'Crazy old Dad'
Wasn't so wrong after all.

Le Gibet (The Gibbet)

The stench of five-dollar perfume
And embalming wine wafting
Around the barfly's sunken eyes
And drooping cheeks held a
Bizarre mystique that I
Couldn't quite place at first.
But her incessant cackling and
Swaying from side-to-side
As she talked to herself
Soon set me to thumping
My foot and humming knowingly.
Goaded by cat-like fascination,
I slipped into her consciousness
Surreptitiously, and together
We conjured sublimely bittersweet
Images of Ravelian desolation:
Her swinging from the gallows ..
And me waiting to cut her down.

Breathless

In the guises of feminism and masculinity,
We paced and stalked definition
With the cunning of a mother lion:
'round and 'round, closer and closer,
until our precarious showdown brought us
face-to-face with insecurity and dream.
As the war-drum heartbeats of a
Million Amazons prepared to vanquish
My masculinity at its first indiscretion,
I loaded my tongue with silver arrows
And mercilessly catapulted the words
'I love you' against your brazen shield.
And simultaneously we fell — breathless.

Retrospective

Over the decades,
Endings muted into beginnings
Like swirls of blue-grey smoke
Creeping toward alabaster palaces
In primordial consciousness.
There, in the garden of creativity,
The ashes of one zillion charred
Impulses rained heavily upon
Furrows of expectations,
Cultivating dreams with experience.

Sea Lines

The ebbing of foam and
Spray from sea lines
Reveals glittering calico
Pebbles and shell fragments
Upon coastal sands.
During the interim of
Drought and abandonment,
The brilliance of this
Treasure trove is dulled
By disclosure and dessication.
There they remain,
Rather indistinguishable
From the multitudes,
And dream of baptism
By tidal reclamation.

Fledglings

Poniard-like buds whisper
Innermost secrets of
Sporophytes and gametophytes,
While fledgling wrens with
Heads pressed close to earth
Listen to the sounds of worms
Inching through sodden humus.
In time, fimbriated foliage will
Scale deciduous boughs in a
Symphony of vascular chiaroscuro
Greenery, rendering refuge
And perch to the weary and
The daring.
Noting the watchful gaze
Of the adolescent feline
In the nearby window,
The mother-wren hurries her
Young onward, explaining
Nothing more than that
Much is to be learned
In a short frame of time.

Imagine

Imagine —
Living in a sanctuary
In some far-off exotic land:
An exclusive enclave where
Hirsute eremites can escape the
Intrusive indiscretions of
The vulgar and the savage.
Mind you —
Nothing too extragavant:
A modest one-room flat
With light maid-service,
A spacious view and, of course,
A state-of-the-art security system.
Just imagine —
It would be a simple life
Of reflection and leisure:
Basking daily in sun and shade
And, when absolutely necessary,
Receiving admiring guests
In true courtly fashion.
(Sigh) —
What do you suppose I
Should call such a place?
Certainly nothing as mundane
As Eden or Elysium.
No, it must be a name as
Enchanting as the the fantasy itself:
Like Gangros .. or Lurana ..
Or perhaps just simply Zoo.

Nighthawk

Primal ritual cries of reveille
From innumerable cricket tribes,
During the wake of nocturnal
Nigrescence, beckon the
Children of Nyx from
Crepuscular seclusion.
A momentary hiatus in the
Mesmerizing rubbing of wings
Divulges the faint slitherings
And slinkings of creepy-crawlers
And creatures of night, in
Exodus from nature's underworld.
And keeping watch over the
Order of things in no man's land
Is a vigilant nighthawk,
Whose stark eyes piercing
Through the darkness stir
Horripilation amongst the meek.

Dirty Talk

Dirty talking shadows in
Dimly-lit, smoke-filled bars
Stir restless gonads to
Suggestion, proposition
And sweet, nasty lies.
The scent of body sweat
Mingles with department store
Perfume like oil and water,
Leather and silk —
Unlikely, yet strangely magnetic.
Oh yeah ..
I love the way the lie
Exuding from your posing stance
Binds my wrists and genitals,
Pulling me to my knees,
Demanding nameless submission.
Across the distance we begin a
Sultry dance of anonymous flirtation:
I turn to catch your stare,
You look away;
My eyes drop to my cocktail,
Yours slowly scan my torso and loins.
I acknowledge with a smile and you
Walk away because I broke the rules,
Was too eager to collude fantasy
With reality and was, therefore, unsafe.
You feign indifference as you watch me
Leave with another two hours later.
And I'm already half-spent as
I prepare to torpedo our dirty talk
Into the bowels of my compromise.

Blade

Our dance is ritual;
A senseless obsession
Between two moths
Playing with fire.
No chains, no whips.
Just bondage … and the
Ever-sweet consequence of
A saber's cutting edge.

Another America

Few Americans know that
The face of Miss Liberty
Is actually that of a
Frenchman's bigot mother.
Like the masses of immigrants who
Yearly forsake old world for new,
We too see majesty of choice
Through all-too-childish eyes:
"Rustler, hustler, bankerman, anchorman,
cop, fag, redneck, punk;
baglady, bastardbaby, stockbroker, chimneystoker,
doctor, lawyer, plumber, drunk."
Yes, we're all watching you,
America .. with Mom's apple pie
On the kitchen table and the
Girl next door at our side.
One nation, trusting in God
Down to our last hard-earned dollar.
"Careful not to step on the crack …
broken backs are hard to mend!"
But the sons of Genet are most
Grateful for the vigilant
Two-in-a-thousand who
Cross the seas frequently
And dream of another
America.

Nocturnal Journey

In the twenty-fifth hour,
As sleeplessness concedes
To Jungian twilight,
The inviolate ticking
Of the bedside clock
Betrays consciousness
With sinister rhythm.
It is a requiem of
Abandonment, whereby
Unprotected souls are
Magically ushered to the
Threshold of time's end.
Clockhands melt into
Surreal images of groping,
Disembodied appendages which
Pull me down into the
Infernal swirling oblivion.
I seem to fall forever;
Plummeting past floating
Sandstone ruins, through
Prehistoric jungles and
At last into a vast galaxy
Of translucent emerald shards.
The heartbeats of innumerable
Still-terrified predecessors
Urge me to scream before
Striking bottom, and I
Awaken in panic: grasping
For the luminous dial
Of my unwitting timepiece.

Spleen

Screeching,
Flamebreathing dragons
Soar low over violated
Plains of brainmatter.
Fires of fear incite
Waves of internal uproar
To sear the ulcerated
Lining of delicate
Abdominal tissue, while
Glowing corpuscles ferry
Hysteria into distended
Veins and scorch alarmed
Nerve endings.
Crops fail, dams break,
Control centers malfunction.
Eyelids clamp shut in
Retreat from the horrors
Of imminent disaster but
Optic darkness is cruelly
Marred by vermillion blotches —
Bits of displaced spleen,
Proclaiming realization of
All that was dreaded yet
Intuited as inevitable.

Razor Roulette

A second's daydream ..
A missed beat in the bass line ..
A slight slip of the blade ..
It felt no worse than a
Mere pinprick but I held
My breath momentarily while
Gazing into the mirror.
My half-shaven reflection
Stared back unexpressively
But no revenge came.
I grinned and lifted the
Razor to my chin again
When suddenly I saw it;
The inky, crimson substance
Seeped and then oozed,
Soon streaking the neck
Of my still-smiling opponent.
Simultaneously we emitted a
Well-known four-letter word
And called an immediate truce.

Cloudburst

Breakdancing clouds
Laughingly roar
With all the grace
Of shattering glass.

Peer Group Heroes

To inner-city true believers,
Average is the ugly consequence
Of weakness and error —
Their idols being tv immortals,
And greatest foe time.
Suitably, peer group heroes
Inspire the less visible
With eloquently-layered lies —
And not once disassociate
Mask from morality.

Dog Days

On dog days,
When nothing goes right,
Impatient young men grumble
That the gods are
Not on their side.
Their pursed lips
May boast indifference
But tell-tale scars
Of self-abuse underscore
The misery of defeat.

Rhythm and Tears

The rhythmic atonalities
Of steely, staccato tears
Pelt graying pigmentation
Almost senseless.
But the romance of flesh
Frozen emotionless by
Half-dried ablutions is
The poetry of endings
Muting into beginnings.

Psyche and Phantasy

Psyche and Phantasy play artfully
At suggestion and intrigue;
Their lovemaking weaves miracles
Through the fabric of dreams.
There, in the Valley of Styx,
Endings mute into beginnings
Like swirls of blue-grey smoke
Creeping toward alabaster palaces
In primordial consciousness.
And soon, the fiery ashes of
One zillion charred impulses
Rain heavily upon furrows
Of creativity, cultivating
Retrospect with expectation.

Le Moment

The way your staring green eyes
Had suddenly bleached to grey;
Your gaping mouth and stiffened muscles —
All frozen into a photographic still;
The stillness of space around us,
Empty of airflow and sound;
All confirmed by the syncopated,
Racing rhythms of my own heart ..
And I knew that the moment had ….

Green

Apples, pears, olives,
Celery, asparagus,
Broccoli, avocados,
Forest trees, emeralds,
Heart chakra, sexy eyes,
Garden snakes, scout uniforms,
Environmental politics,
Army jackets, money,
Greed, jealously —
Green.

When Twilight Comes

When twilight comes and consciousness sleeps in,
Age-old echoes from prehistoric times begin to hum
Ego's cradle-song .. first with low, dark-brown
Cello tones which cause bone-marrow to tremble until
It flows, and then with high, glossy, unheard shrieks
Which can only be made by angels who mean to provoke.
In time, my uneven breathing becomes transformed
Into turquoise-colored waves which whip my oversensitive
Psychic fortress from sobriety, and near panic.
There are no guarantees that I am ready for the
Extraordinary gift that I am to be given:
A glimpse of existence in its unbelievable purity, which
Is so personal that I am forced to grab onto
My earthly reality and smash the perfection
Into countless, cloudy bits of mirror which rain lightly
Upon my consciousness. I awaken sweaty, but not
Completely empty-handed .. and I am not the person
I once had been.

The Homecoming

Two machines work in tandem to
Transport the newcomer to his
Destination: the *Incoming Arrivals*
Terminal, some 60-feet away.
One is called Body; a
Miraculous mechanism of impulses
And veiny cylinders which pumps
Sparks of inertia into otherwise
Lifeless organs and limbs.
Another has assumed the name Escalator:
A complex simple machine, whose
Sleek metal and plastic components
Derive their electricity from a
Brain unaffected by emotion and the
Undependable workings of the spleen.
Together, these two brains scheme
To smuggle Body from plane to
Terminal without arousing its
Potential security risk:
The emotional system.
Body's eye-apparatus fixates
Upon the fourth wall,
Noting neither destination
Nor landscape inbetween.
Brain sends Body impressions
Of Elevator and simultaneously
Commands to "search and find."
Spleen sleeps, sufficiently
Blinded by Eyes (and too
Sophisticated to implement the
Long-since devolved functions
Of Ears and Nose).

Vessels pump … gears spin;
And Eyes notes a multitude of
Peer-bodies assuming similar
Movements; a signal is sent to
Brain, with press releases to
Body: "Everyone is doing it.
Ergo, it must be right!!"
Body moves toward Escalator
With gusto; and Spleen awakens
Abruptly when Escalator
Chuckles "gotcha!!!"
But the hopelessness is not
Fully understood until Spleen
Realizes that Body is alone
In the stream of fast-walking
Zombies, guided by Eyes' robotic
Gaze .. and overhears the one-way
Laughter of Escalator, who
Neither sputters nor flinches.

Don't Ask

Please don't ask me how I am;
You can't really expect
Me to be any different
Than I was yesterday.
We're all really quite normal —
Me, myself and I, and in
Spite of our narcotic state can
Be up and down simultaneously.
And don't look at me too long;
I despise those "I know
How you must be feeling
Eyes" and concerned tone.
Why must you always misconstrue
The way my gaze avoids yours?
My anti-social disposition is
Intended to protect you from us.
No — it doesn't help to
Speak slowly, pronouncing
Each word with the sweetened
Diction of a nun or nurse.
I honestly can't tell you how to
Act, for I have trouble enough
Getting us to agree about
How we'll shield you from me.
It's really best to let me volunteer,
Lest my unbridled demons unleash
Their flame-throwing dragons to singe
The delicate threads of your own ego.
And you, so footloose, must avoid looking
Back into the darkness whose glittering
Maze of mirrors encapture those who poke
Their noses where they don't belong.
Go ahead — ask me how I am ....

Tightrope

I swear they make this tightrope
Thinner each time I attempt to cross.
I remember how my psyche could once
Dance endless sommersaults back and forth.
And how every now and then I would
Laugh mercilessly to myself at how I
Astonished and sometimes even
Infuriated others with my devilish
Dexterity of mind and wit.
But now, having fallen all too often,
I quiver at the sight of both
Challengers and supporters; and
Look upon success in reaching the
Rope's end as another day's survival
Rather than a demonstration of prowess.
I know a good sport never complains but,
I swear they make this tightrope
Thinner each time I attempt to cross.

Saturn's Blues

When the moon is in Fresno
And the sun sets a purplish
Haze over early-autumn skies,
The cold winds of Hell
Breathe heavily against
The hopes of local heroes
And the women that made them.
Farmers stare off into the fields
Without realizing, and housewives
Pull their young close to their
Bosoms — suddenly and
Without explanation.
Intuitively they sense the onset
Of a long and severe influence;
A time of hardship and hindrance
When the faith and courage of
More than a few good men
And women are put to test.
The carousel is out-of-control,
And in the whirlwind confusion
Crops will fail, loved ones will
Pass away, jobs will be lost
And the simplest of dreams will
Be stifled by Saturn's blues:
A mocking nursery rhyme telling
Of horror and despair, and sung
Over and over again with endless
Variations on the same cruel theme.

Some People

Some people long for Spring,
And dream of assuaging the
Bitter sores of Winter's
Darkness and solitude with
Woodland walks and premature
Sojourns to outdoor cafés.
And some people visualize
This year's perfect garden,
An unusually colorful
Palette of vibrant flora
Exploding with hopefulness
And lust for living.
Or rather plan exotic
Summer vacations, June
Weddings and cozy, social
Outings with friends and
Loved ones on traditional
Holidays in April and May.
But others, like me, spend
Year-long winters cuddled up in
Blankets next to the fireplace,
Reading about "some people"
In novels and romance magazines —
With utmost preoccupation.

For the Boys (with Aids)

To friends who don't know
And strangers who don't care,
Soldiers of love worship
Tinsel-town sex goddesses
With all their strength.
They thrive outwardly on
The rantings of Madonna and
Privately soothe their pain
And hopelessness with somber
Strains by Leonard Cohen.
Their greatest ambition is
To shake the shackles of shame
Which imprison and threaten
Them with the most undignified
Fate of all: namelessness.
To some there is no irony in death,
But others are enraged at the
Uncanny plight of these handsome
Living dead whose only crime was
Need for love and recognition.

White Roses

White roses lay neatly placed
Upon the hardened snow —
Just centimeters from where
The still-absent tombstone
Will one day proudly loom
Over wayward leaves, single
Blades of grass and stalwart
Perennials in rainbow shades.
The first tear drools, then
Streams down my wind-burned
Cheeks and others quickly
Follow suit in search of
The meaning of life and death,
As well as other unanswered
Mysteries prompted by your
Almost coincidental passing.
Friends urge me to go on
With my life and speak of
The treasure of memories and
Shared experiences that have
Made me the unique human
Expression that I have become,
And which will further shape
The lives of others I touch.
But i believe in the worms
Which industriously toil at
Converting your precious bones
And ashes to fertile soil which
Will nourish the flowers my
Successors will one day plant
When I, quite coincidentally,
Find the answers you now covet.

POETRY CYCLE 3.

Daedalus : an ancient epic for modern man
an epic reconstruction of the Cretan myths

The Cretan myths

An interpretation by Adam Donaldson Powell

Daedalus' nephew, Talus, was sent to apprentice with him by his (Daedalus') sister. Talus soon rivalled Daedalus as a craftsman and, after some time, Daedalus pushed Talus off the Acropolis in a fit of jealousy. Daedalus was tried for the murder of his nephew and was found guilty by the court of Areopagus. He then fled to Crete to escape his sentence of death.

King Minos of Crete received Daedalus as his master architect and Daedalus performed many feats of engineering and architecture at the king's request. Queen Pasiphae, wife of Minos, befriended Daedalus, and soon confided to him that she knew of his secret history — including the fact that three important inventions that Daedalus attributed to himself (the saw, the geometrician's compass, and the potter's wheel) were actually inventions of his nephew Talus. Pasiphae then proceeded to blackmail Daedalus into helping her fulfill her fantasy of copulating with a magnificent beast named Asterion. Asterion was a champion bull presented to Minos by the sea god Poseidon. (Poseidon, enraged by Minos' refusal to sacrifice the prize bull to him, had sought to punish the king by creating a sexual passion within Pasiphae for the animal.) At Pasiphae's insistence, Daedalus constructed a wooden cow in which the queen could hide herself in order to gratify her passion for the beast. As a result, the queen conceived a son: half-man and half-bull, which came to be known as the Minotaur.

Minos was both outraged and shamed by the existence of the beast and eventually ordered Daedalus to construct an underground labyrinth in which to conceal and imprison it. The Minotaur was situated in the center of the maze of tunnels and corridors, and was fed humans (criminals, pirates, prisoners, the deformed, and the deranged) as its sole form of sustenance.

Shortly after the building of the labyrinth, news came from Athens that Androgeos, Minos' son, had been ambushed and murdered while on his way to Thebes after winning all events in the Panathenic Games. As a result, Minos waged battle against and defeated Athens, thus delivering an especially cruel punishment: seven of the city's young men and seven of its young women were to be sacrificed to the Minotaur each year. Theseus, son of King Aegeus of Athens (and offspring of Aegeus' wife's liaison with the god Poseidon), volunteered to be amongst those chosen for sacrifice to appease the anger of the common people of Athens, who were rioting over the exemption of royalty and the wealthy from inclusion amongst the victims (chosen by an arranged lottery). Distressed by his son's imminent departure, King Aegeus requested of Theseus that, if he should escape and attempt to return to Athens safely, he alternate the color of his sail on the returning ship from black to white as a signal. According to Minoan law, all prisoners were to enter Crete unarmed, but should anyone manage to kill the Minotaur and escape alive, the sacrifice of Athenian youths would be ended.

On the return voyage to Crete, Minos attempted to rape the daughter of Alcathous, King of Megara, who had been taken hostage by Minos, and who also was the cousin of Theseus. Theseus intervened and elicited Minos' anger. After calling each other "bastards", each proved his own divine paternity — Minos by praying that his divine father (Zeus) send a thunderbolt from the skies, which he did; and Theseus by diving into the sea and recovering a gold ring that Minos had moments before seized from him and hurled into the watery depths. Poseidon, god of the sea and father to Theseus, handed his son the ring and Amphitrite (Poseidon's consort) presented him with a golden crown which Theseus wore as he emerged from the water. Theseus then replaced the ring on his finger, to Minos' astonishment.

Before disembarking the ship, Theseus prayed to Apollo and Aphrodite (god and goddess of love) for favor. The gods' gift to Theseus was that Ariadne, Minos' daughter, would fall in love with Theseus at first sight — giving him an insider's advantage over Minos' rule of terror.

As decreed by the gods, Ariadne soon expressed her love to Theseus who pretended to share her passion. Theseus told her that he would marry her and take her away from Crete were he able to escape the labyrinth and death by the Minotaur. Ariadne then consulted Daedalus and tricked him into telling her how a lost person might find his way out of the labyrinth. Daedalus told her that escape from the maze could be achieved by following a trail of thread fastened to the door at the entrance of the labyrinth. On the morning of his surrender to the Minotaur, Ariadne bestowed upon Theseus a clew of thread and a dagger.

Theseus, armed with thread and dagger, left his companions at the entrance of the maze and walked toward the center. He then killed the Minotaur and returned to the entrance, led by the thread. Ariadne released the prisoners and all fled to a waiting ship arranged for by the love-struck princess. Under cover of nightfall, Theseus and his fellow Athenians bore holes in the hulls of the anchored vessels of the royal fleet to prevent pursuit, and they sailed homeward to Athens. On the way, Theseus threw Ariadne overboard off the coast of the island of Naxos, and continued onward to take the hand of Aegle, daughter of Panopeus, in marriage.

When Minos discovered what had transpired, he imprisoned Daedalus and his son Icarus (Daedalus' son by one of Minos' slave-girls) in the labyrinth, expecting that both would perish in the maze, which would soon flood with the rest of the palace as a result of the approaching tidal waves caused by an immense volcanic eruption on Santorini (then called Atlantis). All at the Royal Palace of Gnossos fled southward toward the summer palace at Festos, and deserted Daedalus and Icarus to die in the labyrinth.

Daedalus used wax and feathers to make wings with which to fly, and father and son escaped the labyrinth. Daedalus warned Icarus not to fly too close to the sun as the heat would melt the wax, and not to fly too close to the sea because the sea-spray would weigh down the feathers. They flew northwesterly past the islands of Paros, Delos and Samos, but when they were between the Sporades Islands and the Ionian Coast of Asia Minor, Icarus foolishly flew too high and his waxen wings melted. He plunged headlong into the sea and drowned. Daedalus landed on a nearby island, retrieved his son's body from the waters and buried him. In memoriam, he named the unmarked island "Ikaros", after his son.

Daedalus then flew on to Sicily and took refuge in the court of Cocalus, the Sicanian king of Camicus. By this time, Mycenaen soldiers had burned and sacked the remains of the Minoan palaces at Gnossos, Festos, Aghia Triada, Malia and Zagros, which had already been all but ruined by the sweeping tidal waves caused by the cataclysmic eruption on Atlantis.

Minos, who had escaped with some thirty men, vowed revenge upon the Mycenaens and set out in search of Daedalus, the one man who could help him maneuver a comeback. Minos traced Daedalus by asking all the rulers of the West how to thread a spiral seashell, knowing that only Daedalus, who had solved the riddle of the labyrinth, could possibly know the answer. Daedalus, when presented with this conundrum by Cocalus, bore a hole in the top of a spiral seashell and harnessed the thread to an ant, which proceeded to weave its way through the shell, coming out through the hole at the other end.

When King Cocalus then returned the threaded seashell to Minos, Minos demanded the surrender of Daedalus. After Cocalus' refusal to comply, Minos and his son besieged the underprotected city and took one of Cocalus' daughters captive in ransom for Daedalus. Cocalus then pretended to consent to the relinquishing of Daedalus, and invited Minos to be the guest of honor at a royal feast — Sicilian-style. He also offered the services of his own daughters to assist Minos with the traditional ceremonial bath before the feast. Daedalus, however, had equipped the baths with overhead pipes through which torrents of boiling hot water were passed, and Minos was scalded to death. Minos' men, well plied with wine, food and slave-girls, each had his eyes put out and all were set out to sea on a ship with the body of their dead king. On the helm was painted the crude inscription "Ship of Fools".

Daedalus, homesick for Athens and despondent over his wayward life, succumbed to severe melancholia and committed suicide on the sacred Isle of Delos.

Daedalus : an ancient epic for modern man
an epic reconstruction of the Cretan myths

Act 1

Prologue 1

In the creative tradition
Of cosmic transformation,
The nascence of cognitive evolution
Is precipitated by the yearning of
The soul for individual expression
Through a symbiotic pact between
Science and aspiration.
The juxtaposition of competing
Personal realities within the
Everchanging ethos necessarily evokes
The strategic separation of conscience
And morality within those in pursuit

Of that which makes a legend most.

Prologue 2: Chorus

Thus the universe created
A typology of dieties
To enforce the laws of love
And nature, unknowing that
Human passion for omnipotence
Would sublimate religion
To the glory of invention.
But, for every inspiration
Of genius there is an
Accompanying consequence of
Ignorance; and so it is that
He who constructs a labyrinth
Must invariably suffer confinement
Within the limits of karmic mortality.

Rage 1: Daedalus

Quiet rage kindled by the
Foolish boasting of youth
Provokes restless itching palms
To violent fantasy directed at
The tender ivory pedestal of
Flesh and muscle precariously
Supporting the rose-petal cheeks
And fawn-like eyes of Talus.
The graceful movement of these
Floating, detached hands through
Undefined space and time betrays
The choreography of a nightmare
Unfolding in slow motion;
Ending only when the terrified
Scream of the victim is echoed
By that of the sweating dreamer
And consciousness is restored
Once again.

Murder at the Acropolis

Under cover of night,
The howling of wild dogs and jackals
Forewarns the final waning of the moon
As oily teardrops annoint the marble temple
With glistening treachery.
And in the columnar shadows lurk
The memories of two drunken men,
Pervading silence and open spaces with
Boisterous song and laughter.
The advent of dawn reveals the tearful
Soliloquy of Daedalus, who has succumbed
To the genius of temptation:
"It's so easy to take offense
when one is inebriated ....
Suddenly, everything that has
Ever hurt or angered you
Flashes before your eyes in
Vivid cinematic replay,
And before you know it you're
Struggling for your very life
On the precipice of integrity.
You see, Talus —
I had no alternative but
To do what I did ...
The pain is that it was
So bloody easy."

Daedalus 1: Escape from Athens

Disguised as an unfortunate beggar,
The accused Daedalus loses himself
In a crowded bazaar while awaiting the
Hour of his escape from Athenian justice.
In his cognizant, scientific mind the
Survival of genius irrefutably supersedes
The fallacy of morality and reason
Adjudicated by social acceptability and custom.
And yet, his self-righteous sense of
Confidence and courage are persistently tempered
By the nagging, remote possibility that
He may, in fact, be wrong.

Gnossos

Rising above the Valley of the Mysteries,
Atop the hill known as "tou tselebe he kephala",
Stood the impenetrable and resplendent palace
Of the royal court of Minos.
The photographic reflection of the setting sun
Upon the outer walls of gypsum and lime plaster
Gave the massive structure a brilliant golden sheen,
At once conveying divine favor and prosperity.
And as the stalwart stand of conifers secluding
The fortress from seaward view bowed gracefully
In the warm Cretan breeze, the weary Daedalus
Resumed his slow approach to the north gate
With a muddled sense of hope and trepidation.

Poseidon

Gathering dark storm clouds
Over the southern portion
Of the Aegean Sea signal
The rising anger of the almighty
Earthshaker Poseidon.
The shroud of fear incited
By this ominous omen stirs
Unprecedented hysteria amongst
Panic-stricken birds and livestock
Seeking refuge through flight.
Then, with a sudden lash of
Thunder and electricity, the
Entire Cretan sky becomes
Illuminated with the frightening
Apparition of the laughing god —
Raising his trident in vengeful
Appreciation.

Pasiphae

Feeling like the nigger of the world,
The misogamistic Pasiphae maintains
Self-imposed exile in queenly splendor
Devoid of men and the pain they elicit.
Her god-given lust is neither
Passionate or emotional, for its
Sole motive is womanly revenge
Through bitterness and degradation.

Asterion

On the western grasslands
Appending the palace at Gnossos,
The magnificent Asterion
Snorts and kicks at
Loosened pasture in defiance
Of captivity and civilization.
Amongst the numerous onlookers
Admiring him from safe distance
Is one designing woman,
Who alone can compromise
His nature-given invincibility
Through deceit and manipulation.
Raising his head from the fodder
Of self-involvement, the princely bull
Inadvertently glances at the
Staring huntress and quickly turns
Away in sympathetic embarassment for
Human indiscretion and humiliation.

Daedalus 2: Blackmail

Confronted with exposure
And certain ruin,
The distraught Daedalus
Reluctanctly relinquishes
Allegiance and reason
To the ruthless web
Of hateful nymphomania.
The firey threats of
The desperate queen are
Reinforced by the sadness
Of her eyes, which
Melt the misogyny of
Her accomplice into
Sympathetic submission.
Now joined by the
Mutual exigency for
Challenge and survival,
They endeavor to plot
The seduction of Asterion.

Act 2

Seduction of the Beast

Playing on his
Almost homo sapien instincts,
Pasiphae pursues the beast
With malignant love and deception.
The creature,
Though unstirred by the
Beauty of her dark curls,
Flawless skin and painted eyes,
Is completely transformed
In disposition by
The bovine facade
Of his own illusion.
And somewhere between
Ingenuity and chauvinism,
The priestess and the beast
Unite fatefully;
Each satiated by his own
Conquering phantasy.

Birth of the Minotaur

The priestess Pasiphae lay stretched across the
Stone dais as a prisoner of sacrifice;
Her hands and feet helplessly pinioned by fear
To four-pillar bedposts in surrender to
The fruits of indulgence.
Lightning-like images of horror flash
In vibrant colors against the darkness
Of the night until a momentary calm
Haltingly and mercilessly imbeds upon her
Drunken consciousness one final vision ....
This vision extinguishes all candles
Except for one, and that lone flame
Illuminates the countenance of Adrastea,
The Goddess of Darkness ...
And Death.
From the onslaught of delirium come
Machinations of rape and betrayal in
Rapid succession, spattering the
Whiteness of creation with blood
Of bluish-black and crimson.
The frenzy of violent orgasm overtakes
Her temple, rendering the walls of her
Vagina to tremble as the batterings
Of the wild sea Poseidon rage
Against her malleable shore.
Suddenly, the screams of one thousand
Sirens decry the final exodus of the
Monstrous incubus, and within the
Silence that ensues a new Hell is borne
In the shape of the Minotaur.

Rage 2: Minos

Glaring with disgust and rage
At the repulsive newborn,
The disgraced monarch
Spat and pointed a
Contemptuous finger at
His unfaithful concubine;
Condemning her to a
Sentence of motherhood.
And the attending midwife
Looked away in shame
While the terrified queen
Sobbed in fear and confusion
At the cruel consequence
Of divine possession.

Labyrinth

The curious citizens of Gnossos
Looked on with shuddering relief
As ten palace guards dragged
The struggling Minotaur through
The intricate structure of
Interconnecting passages to his
Barren chamber of confinement.

Vengeance 1: Athens

Standing amid the smouldering remains
Of defeat and destruction was the
Commanding chief of the Royal Minoan Army.
The mandate he delivered to the dreading
Audience conveyed the barbarous and
Bizarre vengeance of King Minos
For the murder of his son:
"From this day … and each year henceforth,
seven of your young men and seven of
your young women will be sacrificed to
the Beast upon selection by lottery."

The Lottery

Above the rancorous protests
From the dissenting crowd
Was heard the martyring
Proclamation of Theseus —
In courageous appeasement.
A resounding cheer
Of victory and approval
Roared across the square
As the bewildered king
Stared at his son in
Shock and disbelief.
In the ensuing moments came
The supportive commitment
Of thirteen men and women;
Volunteering in the heroic
Spirit of Athens.

Aegeus

Masking his sorrow
With kingly decorum,
The despondent Aegeus
Grieves the departure
Of his only son
With tacit consternation.
Upon the painful advent
Of final embrace
The swollen eyes of
Both men rain a
Sprinkling of teardrops
In bidding of courage
And divine favor.
Biting his upper lip
In defense from effusion,
The young prince turns and
Embarks the waiting ship
Without once looking back.

The Rape of the Daughter of Alcathous

Purity of white fleshes outward
With the subtlety of wind chimes
Swaying lithely in the seabreeze …
Sublime fragrances of jasmine and
Virginity meld unwillingly
With sweat and fear
Engendered by threat of violation …
The scent of victimization
Only encourages animal passion and
Further increases the value of the prize …
Beauty — inviting — passion —
Creating — revulsion — increasing —
Attraction — begetting — fear —
Maximizing — passion …
Contorted faces and war-drum heartbeats
Distort humanity as minds are
Dismembered by occlusion …
Peace cannot prevail until
A victor is crowned and
Reintegration is impossible until
Silence shreds its hostility.

Miracle 1: Thunderbolt

In a concerted attempt at
Proving his divine paternity,
Minos closed his eyes and
Raised his trembling arms
Toward the realm of Zeus
Until the mounting force of
Concentration released a
Deafening bolt of thunder to
Burst forth from the heavens
And puncture the pustule
Of scepticism.

Miracle 2: The Ring

Tension was keen amongst the spectators
As all anxiously awaited the questionable
Resurgence of Theseus from the aqueous depths.
But doubt soon turned to astonishment as the
Beloved son of Poseidon defiantly resurfaced
Onto the starboard deck sporting a wry smile,
A golden ring and a gilded wreath of lilies
Bequeathed him by the fair mermaid Amphitrite.

Act 3

Theseus 1: Appeal

Lulled by the gentle
Cradling of the waves
And the soft shimmer of
The early morning moon,
The sleeping ship coasts
Upon the foamy crests
In dreamy quietude.
The insouciant reverie
Is dutifully maintained
By the mesmerizing
Tonalities and rhythms
Of creaking planks
And ocean spray.
And keeping sole watch over
Survival and expectation
Are a lunching rodent
And the insomnious Theseus,
Kneeling in silent supplication
To the celestial guardians
Of love and beauty.

Ariadne 1: Infatuation

Today, Mother Goddess,
I fear that I fell quite foolishly
In love with an extraordinary new
Slave-attendent bearing wine.
No sooner did I take but one sip
Than the resplendent face of Theseus
Captivated both vision and dreams.
I swam in the cool underwater grottos
Reflected in his emerald eyes,
And basked in the dawning borne
Of his sweet parting lips until
The brightness of his celestial smile
Broke my reverie and I found myself
Scampering about on my hands and knees,
Retrieving my fallen cup and
Blotting the runaway wine from
His perfect feet, while stammering:
"I'm terribly sorry ....
I thought you were someone else."

Theseus 2: Thread and Dagger

Armed with clew of thread, dagger and
An invincible strength of purpose,
Theseus of Athens stealthily winds
His way through the maze of dark
Corridors cluttered with hair,
Excrement and mortal bones in search
Of the beast known as the Minotaur.
Verily, the Mother Goddess shakes
Her head in disapproval and shame,
For beasts and the imperfectly-formed
Have a special place amongst the
Beloved of her Kingdom.

Death of the Minotaur

Writhing and moaning
With human-like expression,
The innocent offspring
Of passion and lust
Succumbs to nonexistence
Without knowing why —
Sacrificing his presumptuous
Right-to-life in deference
To the overriding popularity
Of physical beauty
And social convention.
And in his confusion of
Pity, revulsion and respect,
The valiant young Theseus
Replaces the blood-soaked
Dagger into its sheath and
Closes the distended eyelids of
His disabled opponent in combat.

Escape from Gnossos

Stealing through secret passageways
Past sleeping palace guards,
Bare-breasted Ariadne leads Theseus
And the thirteen to safety
With feminine will and insight.
Her pride of success is tarnished
By the inexplicably strange feeling
That she is seeing her past and
Intended future for both
The first and last time.
As she glances back briefly
Upon the impenetrable dormant fortress,
A vagabond tear stains the kohl
Outlining her eyes and she quickly
Turns to resume her traitorous mission
Into the betraying clutches of loneliness
Known only to women who bleed for love.

Ariadne 2: Jilting at Naxos

With the passage
Of a single cloud
Over the persistent sun,
The image of a victim of
Psychological rape is
Eternally engraved upon
The chronicles of history —
As tearing out her hair with
Contorted face and gaping mouth;
And the incessant wailing of
Passionate desperation yields
To rage as the near-drowned
Nymph crawls from sea to land
In a half-hearted attempt
At survival.

Changing of the Sails

The appearance of the Port of Pireaus
On the horizon transforms mirage into reality
As the vagabond ship rocks steadily between
The waves on the 27th day of summer.
Burning rays of sunlight fuel the fervor
Of moving muscles on bare-backed men
Hoisting ropes and alternating sails
From black to white, thus signalling
Their triumphant return from the
Grasp of death into the bosom of victory.
And at the helm stands the young hero Theseus,
Staring without seeing and smiling with
Non-expression: his concentration is
Distracted by the solitary image of a
Young woman in love, screaming his name
In vain.

Cataclysm

Sudden panic on the island of Atlantis
Is precipitated by intestinal gurgling
Within the volcanic cone of Mount Thira.
The impending cataclysm evokes terror
And fear amongst priests and sybarites alike
As the end of the world becomes self-evident.
In a final gesture of prayer and submission,
The doomed hostages of angry gods and nature
Kneel before images of the Great Mother
With fists to brow while the riotous movement
Of bubbling lava and gases escalates into
A hysterical danse macabre to-the-sea as
The earth is purged of decadent overindulgence.

In-flight

Father and son fly high above the
Spray of the sea in an attempt
To escape fatidic injustice through
Science and romanticism.
The synchronous flutter of waxen wings
On these daring charlatan-birds denotes
An intentional defiance of nature,
Punishable by death or evolution.
And so it is, with destined irony,
That the triumphant exhilaration at
Conquering the elements is necessarily
Moderated by mourning and sadness
At the realization that life as known
Can never be the same again.

The Drowning

.... And the scribe of the gods
impartially observes for the
annals of history:
"Daedalus looks on with helplessness
and horror as the youth is pulled
into the blue-green depths and
consumed by the jowls of destiny."

Act 4

Daedalus 3: Elegy

Icarus, my son —
In all honesty I guess we were
Always walking on the edge.
Suspended tautly between highs
And lows, we feared mediocrity
More than imbalance.
For us, challenge was but
The means of attaining individuality;
A space unto ourselves and
Forever out of reach of
Those who dreamed but
Never dared to risk.
We soared like eagles and
We fed on desires that
Sting the heart, yet
We neither gave nor received
Beyond our passion for
Excellence through solitude.
And now that I have witnessed
The birth of my conscience,
There remains no other recourse
Than to reinvest myself in
The ongoing saga which is the
Phenomenon of life.
Heretofore, I'd always thought
That phenomenon is emptiness;
But having now lost all
That has been dear to me —
I realize that emptiness
Is a kind of phenomenon.

The Riddle

Leading the procession of
Thirty haggard mercenaries in
Tattered finery was a short,
Dark-complexioned man with
Dirty black curls and a
Glint of twilight and
Magic in his eyes.
The demeanor of this
Broken-down gypsy with
Affectations of pomposity
And courtly grandeur incited
Both laughter and suspicion
Amongst the curious Sicanians.
Yet — his fixed smile and
Piercing gaze betrayed nothing
But charm as he extended his
Palm holding a simple spiral
Seashell, and said:
"I'll bet <u>you</u> can solve this riddle!??"

Vengeance 2: Sicily

King Cocalus was taken by surprise
In the twenty-fourth hour when
Minos and his band of thirty
Burst into the royal bedchamber
Armed with torches, swords and
A dagger positioned against the neck
Of the fair princess of Camicus,
Held in ransom for he who
Solved the riddle.
Looking into his frightened daughter's
Eyes, Cocalus knew at once that the
First battle had been lost but
Conceded with a smile as his
Bitter mind was already scheming
At a plan for final victory.

Minos

In an expression of growing impatience,
The disapproving gods comment with a sigh:
"Must we be continually aggravated
by these shadows of a man
of stature and consequence,
now diminished into comic parody
by desperation and delusion?
The truth is that no one
Really cares about a star
That has lost its shine ..
A king without a kingdom is
Either a pirate or a buffoon."

The Scalding

The slow dripping of water
Upon blistered skin and flesh
Stages the final element of torture
For the deposed king as each
Drop threatens to erode more
Permanently all hope for
Recovery and revenge.
Melodic shrieks of agony
Maintain symphonic balance
Against the rhythmic trickling,
Indicative of the ironic horror
Endemic to nature's inevitable
Triumph over civilization
And artificiality.
Perhaps the greatest severity
Is the cruelty of mortality;
For chronology minimizes
Individual humanity with
Each passing moment.

Daedalus 4: Lament for a Dying King

It shatters me to see you
Lying there so helplessly;
Playing the 'waiting game'
Without judgment or choice.
Fearing life now more than death,
You transcend the impatience of desire
Through constancy of pain and
Resignation to the inevitable.
In a singular gesture of compassion,
Your pale lips force a smile
Which silences the teardrop
Skidding down my face; and
Momentarily I turn away inside myself,
Embarassed by my own self-indulgence.
Still smiling,
You take me by the hand and
Squeeze a bit of your precious life
Into mine, as if to say:
"I know … I know …
(we all live on borrowed time)."

Ship of Fools

Guided by the constellations
On a voyage to nowhere,
The shattered wealth of the
Heroic age is now overshadowed
By madness.
All blood runs cold
On this ship of fools;
And yet, the vibrant calm of
Heavens and sea remains undisturbed
By the cacophonous wails and
Shrieks of agonized men
And impatient birds of prey.
Verily, the hand of Fate
Is severe with those
Who are slow to acquiesce;
For death without release
Is Hades itself.

Daedalus 5: Eulogy

Beatific phantom choirs of deceased souls
Sing blood-curdling hymns of praise
In honor of Daedalus, who has plunged a
Silver dagger into his own heart
With poetic indifference.
The shrill tonalities of their electrifying
Strains split open the Mount of Artemis
With seismic precision, thus allowing
The corpse to be consumed within the
10-foot crevice without indulgence.
As the rapidly approaching darkness expunges
Temporal expression of irrationality,
Gentle warm breezes over the sacred
Isle of Delos cradle existence
Once again to primal order.

Epitaph

Situated on a hil overlooking
The ruined temple at Delos
Lay a mound of earth covered
With herbs and wildflowers.
Anonymity and olive trees
Shield the unmarked grave
From further disturbance
By inquiry over time.
From the beach below one
Can sometimes visualize
The crescent moon posing
As luminous horns of consecration
Hovering above the burial site —
A symbol of both the old religion
And infinity.
And reflected in the perfect
Scheme of constellations is
The haunting warning of an
Ingenious soul that will
Never rest:
"Ariston metron" …. (moderation is best) ….

Ad Infinitum

The legacy of Daedalus
Is a lesson in pathetic empiricism —
The liability to suffer is a concept
Borne through the fallacy of genius.
Whether he existed beyond the realms
Of mythology and imagination is
Irrelevant; through him mankind has
Inherited the irresistible urge for
Pathos through technology.
It has long been decreed by the Fates
That as Atlantis declined, so shall
Crete … and Assyria … and
Babylonia … and Egypt … and
Macedonia … and Rome … and ….
The carnage is reflected incessantly
Through this hall of mirrors that
We call history, for behind every
Great lust for significance lurks
A Daedalus

POETRY CYCLE 4.

Notes of a Madman

... and as we continuously redefine our identities to ourselves, we persistently turn away from the only reality we know — that we are but the aggregate of the perceptions of others ...

Notes of a Madman

Cast amid a sea of conjecture
Seething with mysterium and magic,
I unleash upon my psyche
The distorted phantasies
Of an undisciplined soul.
Seduced by the romanticism
Of a gibbet in darkness,
I sally past the contingencies of reality
In pursuit of divine retribution,
And aspire toward that which
Must be accepted on faith alone.
My words warrant neither explanation
Nor restraint,
For the notes of a madman
Are understood by his own kind.

Hyacinth

Each Spring,
Appolonian tears of lamentation
Collect as sanguine dewdrops
Upon the verdant slopes of Olympus.
Nurtured by the glory of the elements,
The resplendent rebirth of Hyakinthos
Is made manifest throughout the four quarters
In carillons of sapphire blossoms.
The petals of these bell towers
Cense the air sublime with
The Spirit of the Great Mother
And the legend of creation.
In memoriam, the fugitive solar discus
Lay forever fixed in the heavens
As a symbol of love made Divine
Through resurrection.

Truth is a Whore

Surely, Truth is a whore in ambush;
Scenting the trail of the seeker
With anticipation and illusion.
Quite unashamedly,
She splays her loins to reveal
Treasures of Self-discovery
To the passionate.
Feasting ravenously upon the carnage
Of words and revelations,
The believer plunders the Bitch
With lustful satisfaction.
Ah, but how content he is to
Finally conquer Truth.
For now that she has been impregnated
By Judgment, he may possess
Ignorance more completely yet.

The Zen of Sorcery

The highest magician
Has divined that
The mystery of the veil
Behind the veil
Is revealed through
The bloody consecration
Of his very desire.
Scourged by the beauty
Of the Names,
He salutes the dagger
Of severity
In ecstatic anticipation of
The Angel of Death.
As all light is borne
From the Darkness,
So is the illusion of Hades
Exposed but through Resurrection.
In this way,
The countenance of Isis herself
Is unmasked to all
Who suffer under oath.

Spleen

It seems but yesterday
That love babbled forth so freely;
Undaunted by the doubt
Now rendering me self-conscious
And defensive.
How could a friendship as
Assured as ours yield
To such anguish?
Aieee, the reality hurts
More than the loss;
For in truth,
I've loved not you …
But my perception.

The Chalice

Behold! For within the Great Rite
Lay the mystery of the chalice;
Swept upwards upon the wings of
Divine love and victory,
We consume the Spirit
And re-unite with the Source.
Verily — I am Rhea,
I am the Minotaur …
I am the Chalice.

The Abortion

The stillness of the room is
Gently broken by the first stroke
Of the young concertmaster's baton.
Onstage, the unfolding curtain of flesh
Slowly reveals the
Rising stamen of Ganymede.
Life force swells: the crescendo é accelerando
Of aching muscles and rallying corpuscles
Soon cheer on an intimate pas de deux
Between hand and penis.
At once, the ritual fountain catapults
Stars and comets in a
Grand feu d'artifice.
How suddenly the triumphant applause of
Body and emotion dissipate into silent shame
As the youth wipes away the seed
Of the aborted fetus.

Absurdities of Perception

To gain freedom from absurdities of the Mind,
I count my footsteps
(so silent and arhythmic)
upon the wet sand.
The crash of the waves is muffled by the
Stillness of the dunes;
The saltwater anesthetizes both
Nostrils and swollen feet.
I scavenge the dusk-lit shore for
Lost treasures of memory, while
A solitary falcon-gull scrys
The abandoned abodes of crustaceans.
One-by-one, all impulses of my brain
Coagulate into one thought:
"You will never know yourself until you
become indifferent to the search."
The jeering laughter of the gull
Shatters my Revelation, triggering
My teeth to chatter in
The now-felt cold.
In vain, I retrace the shoreline
In search of my impressions, but
All existence has been cannibalized
By the froth of the moment.
Truly, my absurdities of perception
Are a source of refuge:
The complacency of the sage
Is the bane of the common man.

Mirror of Darkness

Quite enraptured by my own image
In a mirror of Darkness,
I abandon both reflection and shadow
For a glimpse of the Unknown.

The night offers no refraction other than
The glint of an inner eye:
Yea, the paradox of Blindness is revealed
Through discovery of Self alone.

Rite of Passage

Tonight, my Gwion,
I am your Guardian of Sleep.
After performing pagan rites
Of love and devotion,
You asked if I believed
In commitment.
I analyzed the motives
Behind your question,
And circumvented all emotion
In my response.
Through meditation on the Goddess,
We traversed the abyss of Uncertainty:
You, upon the tides of somnambulism;
I, on the wings of wakeful reflection.
Together,
Before the Temple of Minos,
We lay among the ruins of remembrance;
You felt in my caress your vision, and
I saw in you my own image.
We who are bound by the Mysteries
Have always been lovers through Destiny.
And so it is … with commitment …
That I kiss you and
Whisper at the appointed hour:
"Wake up my darling,
It's time to get ready for work."

Anno humanae salutis
(in the year of man's redemption)

How deceptively do glittering lights
In the new city of canyons
Conceal the corset of desperation
Embodying man's faith.
A society of barren undines in
An Elysium of our own fabrication,
We flee the curse of Nostradamus
Through indulgence and invention.
Is it not written that
In the year of man's redemption,
What were once vices
Will then be customs?
There is no escape from Time or prophecy
Except in the play of the mind.
And yet in denial of death
Lay forfeiture of Salvation.

Agitations of the Heart

Overcome with
Agitations of the heart,
The uninitiated seek reprieve
From discontent
In reason
Savored with hope.
They exploit the indulgence
Of rollercoaster emotions
Through passions of purpose
And obsessions of regret,
Thus ensnaring themselves
In the satisfaction of justice.
How can they help
But misinterpret
The vacant smile of the madman
Who finds solace
In the continuum
Of the Great Compassion?

Hieros Gamos

Longing to be raped of humanity
Through possession by the Gods,
The priestess Lexa dances the
Ancient sacred ritual
Like a bitch in heat.
Writhing in the pattern of Uroboros,
The eternal circle of One,
She raises the power and rebirths
In the womb of the
Mother of Darkness.

Void of Course

On rainy nights
When the moon is void of course,
Our eyes are like two strangers
Touching for the one thousand
And first time.
Seduced by my own reflection
In your unyielding gaze,
I glance at myself ...
And then turn away
In acquiescence to the uneven tides
Of my hesitant heart.
I recede into solitude
Where I hold myself until the
Movement of the moon breaks my sleep,
And lubricates my outer Self anew
With tears of reunion.

The Archetypal Kouros

Seated before the altar
At the Minoan Palace of Knossos,
I drink thirstily from
The chalice of Divine Essence.
The intoxication I attain
From the nectar of sacrifice
Tightly binds the
Scrotum of my devotion,
And demands unconditional surrender.
Finally,
As the relentless frenzy
Of my invocation
Reaches an orgiastic climax,
I both consume and
Give birth to myself
In generous libation.

I A O

The Archangel Sandalphon
Reprimands human disillusionment
With compassion and vision,
For the enlightenment of Malkuth
Is reflected in the veils of Tiphareth.
It is through meditations
Of the heart that we encounter divinity;
The voice of the Great IAO echoes
Even from a stone:
"Remember that I have never forsaken you,
I am everywhere."

The Eye of the Triangle

Lost in the assertion that
There is no god but God,
The drunken darwish is
Rendered ecstatic by the
Soma of perfection ...
"la ilaha illa Llah ...
illa Llah ... Allah!" ...
Thus, through the magic of Zekr,
Does the Serpent
Unite with the Regenerative Spirit
And transgress the mundane.
The secrets of the
Unwritten runes within
The eye of the triangle
Are deciphered solely through
Meditations of the heart;
And the rays of initiation
Illumine the paths
Of those led by
Nothing more than
The promise of Salt.

The Coming

On the twelfth day of Bacchion,
The god of magical grace and rapture
Is summoned from the sea
By those willing to suffer to learn.
All hearts on Mount Parnassus are inflamed
By the scent of burning ivy and vine
As the nymphs of Nysa imbibe of the
Ecstasy of madness and destruction.
"Come to us, Thyonidas,
beloved of bacchantes and panthers …
Join us, O nocturnal one,
In our sacred rites."
The frenzy at the Festival of Thyia
Is soon stilled by the prophetic Great Whispering
And the miracle of wine,
Which herald the coming of Lord Dionysus.
Dripping with libations of honey and bloody flesh,
The sated god smiles,
For lifeforce itself is borne
In the womb of pleasure and pain.

And finally ... a little horror

Useless Occupation

Benjamin Friou — Journal Entry, March 1, 1989

Computer Disk Number 54; file name: Spring '89

Well, well ... last night was certainly an interesting evening. Evelyn Waterson, of "Evelyn finally got the nerve to divorce Charlie Atkins" reknown, rang me up out of the blue around 4:15 p.m. yesterday afternoon. Caught me quite off guard — I hadn't heard from her for about a year-and-a-half; only heard stray rumors concerning her 'strange' intrigues. Anway, we had babbled and gossipped for some forty-five minutes when I told her that I would love to talk more but simply couldn't because my ear was painfully sore from clinging to the telephone receiver. Of course, being the same old Evvie underneath the new garments of time and change, she took me quite literally and emphatically insisted that I meet her for drinks in the East Village: "and while we're at it, why not dinner as well. I'm simply starving and I have <u>so</u> much to tell you!" And tell me she did. Although, I must say, she seems to have gotten over the break-up with Charlie completely, and made not one accusation or snide comment. We ate at <u>Ciao Manhattan</u>, a new and trendy "bistro" with good food, high prices and .. do I need to say? .. a tacky name. By the time her dessert came (I was just drinking at that point) she began to tell me about her new friends: a couple of actors, a recent graduate from Harvard Business School, a homeopathist, a Neo-Post-Modernist (?) painter, a cashier at "East-West Natural Foods and Minerals" who was, as she put it 'absolutely, exquisitely cute', and a trance medium (she called him a "channeler") named Winfield Persons. I expressed polite acknowledgment of the former several personalities, but goaded her into telling all concerning Winfield Persons. He sounds quite interesting, actually. She met him at a "Gems and Minerals" show at the Coliseum last January, and they've apparently struck up quite a friendship. It seems that Evelyn has 'gotten into' psychic and occult investigations, and Mr. Persons has given her much guidance and teaching; some of it through channeling. I asked Evvie whether she thought that Mr. Persons would agree to a meeting and/or demonstration of his talents with me, as it sounded like a great angle for a magazine series — perhaps an interview with the the "channeler" followed up with one, or several with the "channelee". Evvie thought it was a wonderful idea and told me she would call Winfield to inquire, but corrected my terminology: a 'channelee' is called a "focalizer". <u>Focalizer</u>? Hmmph! But I took it in stride of course, and departed a little intoxicated (if not thoroughly "ripped to the tits") and in a festive mood. God, do I need a few special themes for features right now! These goddamned movie reviews I've been living off of lately are driving me up the creative wall.

<u>Benjamin Friou — Journal Entry, March 12, 1989</u>

<u>Computer Disk Number 54; file name: Spring '89-1</u>

At the bottom of a pile of bills, junk mail and postcards from my mother (she's gone to Florida again) today, was a note from Winfield Persons. I didn't recognize his name at first, but his business card, which was included, identified him as a "channeler". Then I remembered him as Evvie's friend. She had called him and told him about my interest after all. The message was brief: "Dear Benjamin Friou, I have received word of your interest in my work and would be happy to make an appointment with you for next week. My card is enclosed. Sincerely, Winfield Persons." I read the letter several times, smoked a cigarette while groaning over the bills, and dialed his number. An answering machine with a pleasant message and spacey music urged me to leave my name and number for a return call. He called me back while I was editing a review of <u>Some Like It Hot</u> (a ghastly Madonna remake). We arranged an appointment at his place on the Upper West Side for next Saturday at 8:00 p.m. Sounds like a nice guy.

<u>Benjamin Friou — Journal Entry, March 17, 1989</u>

<u>Computer Disk Number 54; file name: Spring '89-2</u>

11:39 p.m. — I just got home from Winfield's apartment, or should I say loft. What a beautiful space! He lives in a huge old converted ballroom, renovated and furnished in minimalist style, with parkay floors, massive windows, antique oriental carpets, Tibetan paintings, and several ceiling-high tropical plants. Although the surroundings were by no means sterile, the pristine cleanliness of the expanse prompted me to remove my shoes in the entrance foyer without even being asked. Winfield is about 34 years old, tall and lean, has red hair and blue eyes, and is soft-spoken. He invited me to sit down in the living room (and get this: on two enormous overstuffed cushions fashioned from Persian rugs which were situated facing one another under a floor-to-ceiling pyramid made of copper rods and quartz crystals); and he brought in a tray with ginseng tea and gotokola wafers. "Gotokola", he explained, "is the food of the elephants, which many attribute to their long life span." I was awed and overwhelmed, to say the least.

He didn't mind my setting up the tape recorder I had brought along, which was quite fortunate as I would have loathed compromising my attention and concentration any more than absolutely necessary. And so we began: first with me asking elementary questions about his life history, work and intentions; and then with him virtually giving me a discourse on channeling, the elemental workings of crystals, gem and flower elixirs, and their impact on present and future scientific technology and world psychic evolution. I'd used two 60-minute cassette tapes and was quite lightheaded when he quietly announced that the session had reached a terminal point at 10:55 p.m. He then asked me when I wished to meet Kerry O'Toole. I looked at him in puzzlement, and he explained that "Kerry" was his focalizer (boy, was I glad that Evelyn had briefed me on that word — but I got the impression that she had told him about my misuse of terminology, because he seemed to have a curious smile and gleem in his eyes when he enunciated 'focalizer'). I mumbled an "Oh, <u>right</u> .. uh, RIGHT! Anytime! When is he, I mean, are you available?" Winfield laughed softly and emitted a smile as radiant as the refraction of light on the crystals surrounding us, while saying: "Let's try for next Tuesday, about 7:30 p.m. We won't know until then, of course, if it fits Kerry's schedule." "Of course?!!" I exclaimed in return. "Do you mean that he doesn't always appear?" "That's right," he answered with a wink, "focalizers come and go as they wish. And when they're here, <u>they</u> are the ones who are basically in control." "I see," I replied, adding: "this should be most interesting." He agreed to the magazine story on him and his work, and assured me that "Kerry" would not reveal anything to me that was to remain secret. I floated back down to my flat in Soho — I was so "high" that I didn't even once complain or groan about the bumpy ride down Sixth Avenue, as I usually do.

<u>Benjamin Friou — Journal Entry, March 21, 1989</u>

<u>Computer Disk Number 54; file name: Spring '89-3</u>

10:41 p.m. — I've been home for about 40 minutes now, and I'm still in a state of shock over my first session with a channeler. I don't know what to write about it yet — it was one of the most amazing things I've experienced in my entire life to-date. Was it real? I can't say for sure, but it was one helluva impressive show! "Kerry" appeared after some minutes and <u>overtook</u> the body and personality of Winfield completely! Winfield's mannerisms, voice, accent and inflections — everything — were totally transformed into that of a turn-of-the-century gentleman of Irish descent. He introduced himself as "Kerry O'Toole", born in Dublin, Ireland on September 3, 1899 of Scott Edward O'Toole and Hattie Leary. He was a chemist who emigrated to America in 1922; married Antonia Garfield a year later (who ran off with another man afterwards); and he died in New York City, on March 16, 1947 — a recluse and occult scientist — as the result of a "miscalculation in scientific judgment", which he refused to explain or elaborate upon. He told me that he had much to teach me regarding techniques for psychic development and expansion, which would benefit me and the human race at-large. He added that, should I consent to his extraordinary tutelage, I would also give him the opportunity to continue his own previous work through me. When I asked him whether he approved of / or objected to my proposed magazine story(ies), he chuckled and replied that such matters were irrelevant, saying: "If you insist on writing, I will help you — but I've always considered it to be, as Henri Regniér so well coined the phrase, 'a useless occupation'." That was the last thing he said to me before Winfield Persons began to shake all over, and eventually retook control of himself. He didn't say much after that, other than that he was always exhausted after a channeling session, remembered nothing of what had transpired, and did not particularly wish to know either. My dealings with Kerry were not his personal concern. I played back Kerry's invitation to me for continued communication, and we set up a schedule beginning with the following Saturday evening. And then he politely hurried me to the door. He looked truly ill, but I guess that I would feel out-of-sorts myself had I been through such a psychic upheaval.

<u>Benjamin Friou — Journal Entry, March 29, 1989</u>

<u>Computer Disk Number 54; file name: Spring '89-4</u>

1:04 a.m. — Tonight's session was most fascinating. We covered several esoteric and scientific principles, including telepathy, the psychic impact of color and sound, the etheric planes, and the precepts of alchemical research. Kerry is amazing. He knows exactly when to stop so that I don't overload.

<u>Benjamin Friou — Journal Entry, April 12 1989</u>

<u>Computer Disk Number 54; file name: Spring '89-5</u>

Over the past couple of weeks I've become increasingly obsessed with my studies. I've stopped socializing entirely — most of my time is consumed with wading through rare volumes on physics, geometry, mineralogy, and theology at Columbia University and the New York Public Library. I've left the telephone disconnected the past several days. Kerry has been very encouraging and patient, and assures me that I am making commendable progress. One thing he said tonight puzzles me though: he said that the time is soon coming when it would be more expedient for him to come to me, rather than for me to come to him. I didn't really understand, but I didn't question him any further on the matter either. I've learned to judge what is to be merely accepted by the tone of voice he employs.

<u>Benjamin Friou — Journal Entry, April 27, 1989</u>

<u>Computer Disk Number 54; file name: Spring '89-6</u>

8:21 a.m. — A very sad and disappointing morning, indeed. Evelyn just called and awakened me with some rather disturbing news: Winfield is dead! His sister found him lying in a pool of blood in his kitchen last night. He had plunged a dagger through his own heart. No motive has been established. I feel awful about it — poor Winfield! Poor Kerry! I never once considered this as a possibility; nor did I ever stop to realize how dependent I (we) were upon Winfield. It's hard to believe it is all over. So <u>suddenly</u>! I'm depressed.

<u>Benjamin Friou — Journal Entry, April 28, 1989</u>

<u>Computer Disk Number 54; file name: Spring '89-7</u>

"Dear Diary:" I feel like a young girl in love! The most wonderful thing has happened. I was so depressed after Evvie's phone call yesterday morning, that I remained in bed all day and all night long. I awoke around 4:00 a.m. this morning with a migraine headache and a strange ringing in my ears. I had trouble rousing myself out of my somnambulance and, indeed, remained in a sort of half-conscious stupor. I felt moved to get out of bed and find pen and paper in order to write. What I was going to write, I had no idea — but the pull was very strong. After an unaccounted amount of time I heard the ringing in my ears return, my dizziness lessened, and I looked down at what I had written. The writing was in a foreign script — an almost unintelligible scrawl, if you will — but it clearly read, to my astonishment both then and now, "Winfield Persons has succumbed to obsolescence; Kerry O'Toole lives now more than ever. Keep paper and pen by your bedside. You will find it to be of convenience. (signed) Kerry O'Toole." My hands were trembling as I reread the paper over and over again. So <u>this</u> is what he meant — automatic writing! I've been up for three hours now, and it still feels like a dream.

<u>Benjamin Friou — Journal Entry, May 15, 1989</u>

<u>Computer Disk Number 54; file name: Spring '89-8</u>

I've stopped thinking about the magazine series for now. All the editors I've queried have given me a polite "We feel that market is not ready for the topic" or "Perhaps, we could use a short story — but purely as fictional entertainment." I get the feeling that most of them think I'm mad. It's just as well, I guess. All I really want to do now is continue my studies with Kerry. Even my personal journal entries are becoming less frequent. Up until last week I had been copying the automatic writing by hand and then transferring it to computer disk. As Kerry has been feeding me data in one and-a-half hour sessions, three times-a-day, daily — I've had to stay up half the night retyping it into the personal computer. But now I've begun taking the dictation directly onto floppy disk. Kerry is quite pleased, as I'm less tired, have more concentration, and we're getting more work accomplished. He has humor indeed: two days ago he prefaced an essay on mummification and life suspension with the salutation: "Dear Ghost Writer,". But Kerry is also quite practical. He forces me to take the necessary time out to do the blasted movie reviews — even though I'd rather not be bothered. And he pushes me to exercise and eat well, saying: "A healthy body and mind are indispensible to our present and upcoming work. They are your vehicle for psychic transformation." Transformation — that word again. I understand him, and then I don't .. at least not completely. When I feel frustrated with my progress, he soothes me by admonishing me to be patient with myself, and by assuring me that I will soon know more than even Winfield did. Then he usually makes a joke or finds some other way to make me laugh. For example: last week I had gone to a premiere screening of "Ghostbusters 3". When I returned home, Kerry dictated a wonderful "black humor" review of the film. I commented that I hadn't realized that he had been at the screening. He replied that he hadn't, in fact — but that having access to my mind also meant that he has full awareness of my personal experiences, in as much detail as I sense them myself. I was a bit disturbed by this when he first said it, although I've known it to be the case for quite a while now. Over the past two and-a-half weeks our communications have become much more dialogue-oriented. It's strange to think of how anyone else would react to seeing me sitting for hours on end in front of my computer screen, talking to myself through my typing. Damn! My ears are ringing. I'd better sign off on the journal for now.

<u>Benjamin Friou — Journal Entry, May 27, 1989</u>

<u>Computer Disk Number 54; file name: Spring '89-9</u>

Kerry has me researching more and more religious and anthroposophical texts now. He says he has enough physical science and mathematical input. I've been reading several obscure volumes on Theosophy and secret societies such as the Essenes, Golden Dawn, the early Masons, etc. In addition, he has relayed to me the fruits of his own previous research into the esoteric theories and practices of the early Egyptian priesthood, the Lemurians, the Atlanteans, the Minoans, and the Byzantinians. My mother called and asked why she hasn't heard from me, and why she hasn't been able to reach me by telephone for so long. I explained that I've been working very hard. She's invited me to take a break and join her in the Berkshires for a few days, and then spend the weekend in Boston. She has symphony tickets to hear Ashkenazy play the Brahms 2nd piano concerto. She wouldn't let me say "no" flat out, so I promised to think about it and call her back tomorrow. Kerry has insisted that I go. He says it's time for me to take a little break anyway, and that it's better than her visiting my flat unexpectedly to check up on what's going on. He's suggested that I take two weeks and spend some time in Salem, Massachusetts before returning to New York City. When I asked him "Why Salem?", he responded by saying: "Because of the historical and occult archives, of course." I asked him if he intended for me to start studying witchcraft, and he explained that "witchcraft" is an uneducated term invented by ignorant Christians who lived in fear of the unknown, and which was fostered by greedy members of the inner-Church who did everything possible to keep the higher teachings from the public-at-large. "Witches" were, then, any persons who presumed to go beyond traditional organized religion in faith and practice. He further told me that all major organized religions have similar outcasts: Islam has its Sufis, Judaism has its Qabbalists, etc. The religions that attempted to preserve knowledge in their practices have been either totally annihilated or forced to go underground as secret societies. New Age spirituality, he elaborated, is not actually "new" at all — it is more a rediscovery of practical knowledge long ago employed by the ancients. I'll call Mother in the morning.

Benjamin Friou — Journal Entry, May 28, 1989

Computer Disk Number 54; file name: Spring '89-10

Needless to say, Mother is delighted — as much for having gotten her way after all, as for obtaining my company. I leave for Great Barrington, Massachusetts tonight.

Benjamin Friou — Journal Entry, June 13, 1989

Computer Disk Number 54; file name: Spring '89-11

I'm back. Mother was dreadful — so many questions about my life, my work, my social life, etc. But I think I did a pretty good acting job because she seemed satisfied when I left her in Boston. I told her that I was off to Connecticut for a week-and-a-half to stay at Evelyn's cottage outside Darien. That, of course, pleased her considerably. She's always worried about me working too hard and isolating myself socially. I felt embarassed approaching the historians in Salem about witches at first, but I was received quite unabashedly. It appears that such investigations by scholars and writers are not uncommon. What I uncovered proved most fascinating, in light of my other studies to-date. But, I must admit that I am feeling a bit uncomfortable about where this is all heading.

<u>Benjamin Friou — Journal Entry, June 29, 1989</u>

<u>Computer Disk Number 54; file name: Spring '89-12</u>

Kerry has had me read several books by Annie Besant, <u>666</u> and other books by Aleister Crowley, some writings by Rudolf Steiner, and a curious book called the <u>Necronomicon</u>, which I gather was relayed through automatic writing. He has also been teaching me about visualization, the psycho/spiritual effects of religious and occult rituals, the essential qualities of the four elements (earth, air, water and fire), and various geometrical configurations useful in talismans. His last communication was as follows: "The time has now come to learn the practical applications of the academic knowledge attained thus far. Go thee to the Magickal Mandrake Bookstore on West 18th Street and purchase the following — four white candles encased in glass tumblers, two black candles, an incense brazier, a silver chalice, a package of charcoal suitable for incense burning, an ounce of "Flying Oil", a double-edged dagger, and these herbs: a half-ounce of belladonna, a half-ounce of lobelia, a half-ounce of absinthe … and, oh yes, you'll also need to purchase one large and one small mason jar, a mortar and pestle, six bottles of strong wine, and four large white quartz crystals as well as one smokey quartz crystal, thirteen small pieces of obsidian, and twenty feet one-quarter-inch diameter copper wire. Benjamin," he added, "don't question me on this — just <u>do it</u>!" The last statement was demanding unlike ever before. I don't dare cross him.

<u>Benjamin Friou — Journal Entry, June 30, 1989</u>

<u>Computer Disk Number 54; file name: Spring '89-13</u>

Well — I've made the purchases, as requested. What a strange store, and filled with even stranger things! It's a virtual occult supermarket, frequented by fairly normal-looking people of all ages; and no one flinched at all when I presented my shopping list. I did have trouble figuring out where to buy the crystals and obsidian, but a quick phone call to Evelyn led me to a perfectly-suitable gem and mineral outlet in the East 30's. I haven't heard from Kerry all day. I guess he's giving me a chance to take all this in.

<u>Benjamin Friou — Journal Entry, July 1, 1989</u>

<u>Computer Disk Number 54; file name: Spring '89-14</u>

Blast! Kerry woke me up at 5:30 a.m. this morning, telling me it's time to go to work. He's had me typing all sorts of exercises non-stop for the past six hours — I finally have a break, but who knows for how long. Thank God I have the journal in which to blow off steam. There's certainly no one else to complain to. The exercises and assignments have to do with astral projection, visualization, ritual methods for casting magic circles, instructions for setting up an altar room; recipes for libations and making incense; invocations of spirits, candle magic; and various chants, dances and sexual techniques for creating a magical power source. The first hour and-a-half was spent taking the dictation for the index alone, so I expect that I'll be inputing the information nonstop for days on end. I've only just started on the visualization techniques section.

<u>Benjamin Friou — Journal Entry, July 12, 1989</u>

<u>Computer Disk Number 54; file name: Spring '89-15</u>

I've successfully cast circle a few times now, and Kerry has ordered me to rest all day long. Tonight he will dictate to me special instructions leading up to final transformation. We will conduct the ritual during tomorrow night's full moon. I haven't been feeling so well the past few weeks — not really sick, but generally weak in my body, and I've needed to sleep much more than usual. It's probably just fatigue from all the heavy psychic work I've been doing.

<u>Benjamin Friou — Journal Entry, July 13, 1989</u>

<u>Computer Disk Number 54; file name: Spring '89-16</u>

The ritual went well. I followed Kerry's instructions to the letter, even spilling a few drops of my blood into the libation mixture while invoking the Spirit of Kerry O'Toole. I then visualized the spirit as entering the libation chalice and drank it all. I don't know what happened after that; I must have fainted, because when I awoke I was lying on the floor in front of the altar and all the candles had been snuffed out. Kerry's instructions are to repeat the ritual every Friday night from now until the next full moon. He has promised me that I will feel stronger after the final ritual. I feel nauseous. Almost like I have "morning sickness".

<u>Benjamin Friou — Journal Entry, August 3, 1989</u>

<u>Computer Disk Number 55; file name: Summer '89-1</u>

My headaches have gotten much worse, and I've been having long lapses where I can't remember where the time has gone. Kerry isn't saying much other than that I will feel like a new person after the final ritual. That happens in another week and-a-half. I'm too tired to be enthusiastic about much of anything, but I sort of look forward to getting it over with.

<u>Benjamin Friou — Journal Entry, August 9, 1989</u>

<u>Computer Disk Number 55; file name: Summer '89-2</u>

I've been having a very disturbing nightmare which has recurred for the past three nights now. In the dream I am doing the ritual, but when I draw Kerry's spirit down into the libation chalice i visualize Winfield in the mixture: with a dagger through his heart and a terrified expression on his face. Then he wrenches the dagger from his chest and hands it to me, saying: "It's your only chance .. it's your only chance." I've been waking up in a sweat after every dream. I haven't heard from Kerry since the nightmares have begun. In his last communication he told me that we were soon to meet in the flesh. He seems to be getting stronger and stronger, but maybe it's just that I'm feeling so weak. I don't know. Just a few more days until the blasted full moon.

<u>Benjamin Friou — Journal Entry, August 11, 1989</u>

<u>Computer Disk Number 55; file name: Summer '89-3</u>

I can hardly get out of bed; I'm so weak and depressed. The nightmares haven't stopped. I'm a little worried about getting confused during the ritual tomorrow night because my brain has been like scrambled eggs due to the blackouts and the dizziness. I wake up mumbling to myself too; usually the incantation I say right before i drink the libation mixture: "Come to me, Friend in Darkness. From my life so shall you have Light."

<u>Benjamin Friou — Journal Entry, August 12, 1989</u>

<u>Computer Disk Number 55; file name: Summer '89-4</u>

Benjamin Friou has died, along with Kerry O'Toole, by his own hand. May the Darkness always remain un …… Bbbyye, Mommm….//

****

What Jonny Dug Up

October 15th. Blustering winds scattering leaves and raindrops over lush greenery and displaced benches in Kampen Park. The singing of the breeze through shrubs and trees muffles the occasional sounds of traffic in the distance. Non-constant noises … sloshing of cars through puddles … stalling motors gasping and choking … and every now and then, a shriek from a skidding car, grabbing onto the wet asphalt as if clutching for its life. A quiet night: uneventful. Cold. Empty. The kind of evening most people stay inside, cuddled up beside the fireplace with a long novel. Or rooted in front of the television set, even though not a single program of interest is scheduled for broadcast. Perhaps also the kind of night one could expect to sow the seeds of a common cold, or the flu. Otherwise, a night like any other in Oslo during mid-October. Well, almost ….

I was walking Jonny, my golden retriever, around 9:30 p.m. He seemed to be in no hurry to relieve himself, to my dismay — as I found the weather rather inconducive to a prolonged stroll. After much cajoling on my part, Jonny took an interest in an out-of-the-way shrub that had never attracted him before. Wherewith some excited sniffing and barking, Jonny began to whine and dig at the earth underneath the shrub. The more that I attempted to force him to heel, the more persistent he became. Finally, I figured 'What the hell' — the sooner he uncovered the bone, or whatever it was, the sooner we could finish up the business at hand and return home. And so, I unleashed the dog and lit a cigarette. After digging about a quarter meter into the loose soil, Jonny began to bark and wag his tail anxiously. "Good boy, Jonny," I cried. "Bring it over here. 'Atta boy!" Jonny pulled at what looked like a mass of unravelled brown rope, and began to drag the object toward me with great pride. I was just about to pick up the treasure-find for closer scrutiny, when I began to feel quite nauseous. He had unearthed the severed head of a woman, barely identifiable .. with worms and other insects of the soil crawling about her eye-sockets, ears and mouth. There wasn't a nose — maybe it had already decayed before the rest, but I don't think so. It was a horrible sight!

The next half hour is fuzzy in my recollection. I'm not quite sure how, but somehow I managed to leash up the dog and run to the nearest apartment building. Apparently, I had been quite hysterical .. randomly ringing the buzzers of all inhabitants of the building while screaming and crying. The dog was confused and excited over my madness as well. It took several tenants to get us inside and under control. I must have been babbling complete nonsense, because the apartment-dwellers who telephoned the police thought that I had been sexually-assaulted — although they couldn't understand how that had been possible with such a large dog for protection. The dog and I were sitting in the vestibule, just inside the front door of the building, surrounded by five or six tenants. No one dared to invite us into their homes ... Kampen isn't really the kind of neighborhood where people get too involved in other people's affairs. It's quiet, residential — a no-trouble community.

The two policemen who arrived must have asked me about twenty-five questions about myself before I could get a word in about what I had seen. "What is your name, address, telephone number? Where do you work? Are you single, or married? Why are you walking in the park so late at night? Etc." I was half-expecting them to ask me if I was working as a prostitute, when one of the officers finally told me that the tenants had complained about my screaming, and they would escort me home or to a hospital after I gave them my description of the assailant. By the time I was able to explain to them that I had not been raped, but rather had discovered the partial remains of a probable murder victim, I was so angry that I practically dragged them by the hand to the disgusting head of the poor woman, while pointing and screaming, "Look at that! <u>LOOK AT IT</u>" That was all I could divulge in my state: 'Look at it!' One of the officers led me away from the park, radioed for help, and called for another car to drive me home, explaining that he had all the information he needed from me for the moment. I would be contacted later for an official statement. Once home, I cried .. and cried .. until I fell asleep on the sofa, at God only knows what hour.

I awoke from my troubled sleep with a start. The telephone was ringing, the dog was barking, and the answering machine was signalling that messages had been taken. Half awake, I grabbed the receiver. "Hullo ... Jonny, PLEASE SHUT UP! ... No, I'm sorry .. not you .. the dog. Who's calling?"

"It's Petter," said the voice on the other end. "Are you ill? I've been trying to call you all morning long. Have you forgotten about the shoot, or what?"

"Oh, Petter!" I cried. "What time is it? I must have overslept ..."

"It's 10:37 a.m.," he replied. "We were supposed to meet with the camera and make-up crew at Aker Brygge at 8:30 a.m., remember?!! Are you alright? I don't understand. You've never missed a shoot before, Turid. What's going on?"

My God. I had totally forgotten about the <u>Solo Light</u> shoot. "I'm really sorry, Petter. So much has happened. I guess I was so exhausted that I forgot to set the alarm. But I don't see how I can work today. I need some time to .. I mean .. I just can't do any..."

"Okay, it's okay. Slow down .." he interjected. "I sent the crew home an hour ago. We'll re-schedule the shoot. But you sound terrible — is there something wrong? You aren't hurt, are you?!!"

"Yes," I stammered. "I mean, no .. my God, Petter. I'm a mess!" Starting to sob over the phone: "It was horrible! I can't explain ..."

"Listen, I'll be right there. Stay where you are; and don't do anything. I'll be there in twenty minutes. Okay? I'll be <u>right over!</u>"

"Okay, Petter ... please hurry. I really need to talk to somebody."

After hanging up the receiver, I felt lonelier than I'd felt for a long time. I hugged and kissed Jonny, gave him some food and water, and opened the window blinds. I looked at the clock. 10:44 a.m. Petter will be here soon ... I'd better try and pull myself together. Looking in the bathroom mirror, I saw that I had circles around my eyes, my face was bloated, and I looked pale. "You really look awful, Turid," I said to myself. And with that, I quickly washed my face, threw on a layer of make-up and changed clothes. I had just put the coffee on when the buzzer rang. Petter had arrived at the entrance of the building. In less than two minutes he had bounded up the four flights of the apartment building, and was in the entrance hall to my flat.

"Turid, what's wrong?!! Are you hurt? What has happened?" he panted. And I just broke down and started to sob, all over again — trembling and staining the quick make-up job I had completed just minutes before. Petter put his right arm around me and walked me to the sofa, where he sat me down and held me, saying: "It's going to be okay, now. It's going to be alright."

"Petter, I'm so sorry about the shoot. I didn't mean to ..."

"Don't think about the shoot right now, Turid. It's not a problem. Right now we've got to calm you down. That's all that is important at the moment."

I felt so awkward, weeping like a child in Petter's arms, and making no sense at all. Petter had taken a special interest in me ever since I first walked into the modelling agency, eighteen months ago. He had transformed me from a gangling, self-conscious nineteen-year-old into a sophisticated young woman — at least on the outside. He'd taught me how to walk, how to carry myself in front of the camera and at fashion shows and, yes, even how to make love. I adored his dark hair, deep blue eyes, cleft chin, and broad shoulders. My perfect Petter. Twenty-five, tall, masculine, self-confident ... I cherished so much about my Petter; perhaps too much. I didn't want to get serious with any man now. My career was just beginning. And so it was I who suggested that we break off the sex, and continue as agent/model and as "good friends". Yes, it was very awkward crying in his arms at this moment, but I was damned glad he was here, holding me as he was.

"Can I get you something ... water, a drink?" he asked tenderly.

I wiped the tears from my swollen cheeks, sniffled a couple of times, and replied quietly: "Sure. Maybe a cup of coffee. I just put some on in the kitchen."

"Cream and sugar?" he asked softly, with a reassuring half-smile.

"No .. I'll take it black. Thanks." Jonny had snuggled at my feet and was looking up at me with worried eyes. "I'm okay now, Jonny," I said, giving him a few strokes on his head and back. I surveyed the living room and noted that I hadn't done any of the cleaning chores I had planned to do the night before. The coffee table was littered with newspapers, my half-eaten dinner, and an ashtray overcrowded with cigarette butts. Petter returned with two cups of black coffee.

"Here you are!" he said, handing me one of the cups.

"I feel so embarassed," I blabbered. "I'm a mess, the apartment is a mess ..."

"Yeah, yeah. Just relax now ... and tell me what has happened."

I took a sip of the hot liquid, lit a cigarette, and exhaled a slow stream of blue-grey smoke toward the ceiling. "You're probably not going to believe this," I began. "It was just like a nightmare ..."

"Try me," he said, squeezing my hand lightly and then releasing it.

"Well, last night around half past 9:00 p.m., I was walking Jonny in the park. I was a little preoccupied with all the chores I had to take care of before going to bed, and I wanted to get back as soon as possible since I had an early morning shoot. We were walking on the side of the park closest to the corner of Økernveien and Ensjoveien, when Jonny got all excited and began barking at a shrub. I tried to pull him away, assuming that it was some poor terrified squirrel. But Jonny started digging at the ground with his front paws, and with such determination that I finally just unleashed him to uncover whatever he was looking for. You see, I sometimes let Kåre take him for a walk in the park, and then pay him 10 crowns or so ..."

"Who's Kåre?" asked Petter.

"He's the kid who lives in the apartment below me," I replied. "I thought that perhaps Jonny had buried something there recently on one of their walks together, and now wanted to dig it up again. Anyway, I had just lit a cigarette and was about to congratulate Jonny on his efforts when I realized what he had dug up. I totally freaked out .. it was — <u>absolutely horrible</u>!"

"What was horrible? What did he dig up!" asked Petter anxiously.

"It was a severed head," I blurted. "The rotting head of a woman, I think — with no nose .. and with worms crawling all over her eyes, ears and mouth."

"Oh, no ... oh, Turid!" gasped Petter. "No wonder you're in such a state! Did you call the police?"

"No ..." I replied. "I mean, <u>I</u> didn't — I was too incoherent at first. But I scared the hell out of everybody in a nearby apartment building, and someone there called the police. I then led them to it, and a policeman drove me home. I don't remember much after that, but I must have passed out here on the sofa. I guess I was still in a state of shock and exhaustion.

"I bet you were," replied Petter. "I'm really sorry you've gone through this."

Petter put his arms around my shoulders and nuzzled his face into my hair ... it felt good; <u>very good</u>. I didn't resist, but rather whimpered: "Take me to the bedroom, Petter ... please. I need you now."

I awoke an hour-and-a-half later to find Petter sitting beside me on the bed, smiling and stroking my forehead and hair gently. "Hi," he said. "Feeling better?"

"Hello. I must have drifted off. How long have I been asleep?" I asked sleepily.

"Not long .. I guess about 15 minutes, or so. How is my best model now?"

"Okay, Petter. I ..."

"Don't say anything," he said, interrupting me. "As far as I'm concerned, a horrible nightmare has had a very beautiful awakening."

"Yeah .. it's been a long time." I noted.

"Too long," he replied, giving me a loving peck on my left temple. "Listen, it's now 12:55, and I have a 2:00 p.m. appointment with a client downtown. Do you mind if I take a quick shower here before I scoot off?"

"Of course not," I said. "Go right ahead .. you know the way."

"I can still cancel if you need me to ..."

"No, please don't. Really! I'm fine now," I said, trying to appear cheerful and refreshed.

"Are you sure?" he beseeched.

"Absolutely! Besides, I've screwed up your schedule enough today as it is," I said.

Petter leaned toward my face and kissed me again, saying: "Okay. I won't be a minute."

While Petter was in the shower, I threw on a robe and played back the morning's messages. 8:52 a.m. — a message from Petter. 9:23 a.m. — another message from Petter. 10:10 a.m. — was a call from a Lieutenant Tjæreborg, Oslo

Police Station: "Yes, Miss Alvdal. Please call Lieutenant Tjæreborg at the Oslo Police Station as soon as possible regarding the incident in Kampen Park. Tlf. 22.48.00.35." I sat staring into space for a moment, not certain what to think, and then I nervously picked up the receiver and began to dial. "May I speak with Lieutenant Tjæreborg?"

"Hold on while I page him, please," said the voice on the other end of the line. "And whom shall I say is calling?"

"This is Turid Alvdal, returning his call."

Seconds later, Lt. Tjæreborg picked up the phone. "Miss Alvdal? I'm handling the investigation of the Kampen Park case. I wonder if you could come down to the station and review your statement from last night for us officially — just for the record. I'm told that you were in shock at the time, and I just want to re-confirm the information for the investigation report."

"I guess so," I said, hesitantly. "When would you like me to come down?"

"As soon as possible, if that's convenient," he answered. "Just ask for Lt. Tjæreborg in Room 307. You will be shown the way."

"Okay," I replied nervously. "I'll be there within forty-five minutes."

"That would be fine. I'll be waiting for you."

I hung up the telephone and just sat still for a couple of minutes, staring blankly into space. When I finally looked up, I saw Petter standing over me, drying his hair.

"Everything alright?"

"Yes, fine," I replied. "That was a Lieutenant Tjæreborg from the police station. He wants me to come down and verify my statement from last night."

"Do you want me to come with you? It's no problem, really!"

"No, no. I'm fine. I just have to pull myself together real quick. It's just a routine matter, I'm sure. It shouldn't take but a few minutes," I mumbled.

At two o'clock I was in Lieutenant Tjæreborg's office.

"Miss Alvdal?"

"Yes, and you must be Lieutenant Tjæreborg?!" I responded.

"That's right. Miss Alvdal — if you would be so kind as to read over this statement from last night which we've typed up, and verify the facts and sequence of events."

I read the report twice, cringing both times. "As far as I can remember, it's pretty accurate," I said finally.

"Good .. have you anything else to add? Perhaps something you forgot to mention last night, that you now remember? Anything — even if it seems trivial."

"No, I can't think of anything else," I replied.

"Very well then, Miss Alvdal. If you'll please just sign the statement right here ..."

"Do you have any clues about the identity of the woman," I asked. "... or the murderer? I mean, who would do such a terrible thing?!! He must be a very sick person, indeed!"

"Well, we have found some additional body parts not far from where your dog dug up the head."

I was shuddering as the Lieutenant spoke.

"But so far," he continued, "no other significant clues that would lead to positive identification of either victim or murderer."

I sat back in my chair.

"As for the murderer," he added, "it could be anyone."

I didn't like the way he looked at me when he said that — almost as if <u>even I</u> could be a suspect.

"It's difficult, Miss Alvdal, to get to the bottom of cases such as this one. When the victim and the murderer are involved with one another in some capacity, a motive can be established fairly readily .. and the killer identified. And in cases where there is a trend, we usually catch on pretty fast. But — an isolated incident such as this one — which happened so long ago, and with no fingerprints — well, it's difficult."

I shook my head and said, "I can't understand how anyone could do such a thing .. and to mutilate the body like that!"

The lieutenant looked me straight in the eyes and asked: "Miss Alvdal, have you noticed anyone digging in Kampen Park over the past month?"

"Not that I can recall," I replied.

"Let me ask you something else then," he continued. "How often do you and your dog .. what is your dog's name?"

"Jonny," I answered quickly.

"How often do you and Jonny go walking in Kampen Park? Is it once-a-day, twice-a-day, more? In the evenings, mornings, afternoons ..? And did Jonny run directly to that spot and begin digging up the head, or did he seem to find it by accident?"

"He ran directly, I think .. now that I .. I don't understand what you're getting at Lieutenant," I protested uncomfortably.

"Miss Alvdal, we believe that the woman in question has been dead for about three weeks now. I just thought that you and your dog may have possibly seen someone digging in the park around the time of the murder."

"No. I haven't seen anything like that at all, Lieutenant." Honestly, he made me feel guilty, just by the way he looked at me. "In fact," I elaborated, "last night was the first night we had been to the park for a couple of months."

"A couple of months, do you say?"

"Yes. I've had a very busy work schedule lately, so we've basically just been for short walks around the block."

"I see. Well, thank you Miss Alvdal. I think that will be sufficient. If you should happen to think of anything else, please don't hesitate to give me a call."

I replied that I most certainly would, and left the police station hurriedly, while thinking: 'I hope they catch that sick son-of-a-bitch soon — I'm really getting the willies.'

Afterwards, I took the subway downtown and bought myself a new outfit. Buying new clothes usually makes me feel better when I'm depressed. But somehow, it didn't do very much for my mood this time. On the way home, I stopped in at the Pakistani-owned tobacco store between the bus stop and the apartment building. That's when I noticed the story on the front page of the evening edition of <u>Aftenposten</u>. "Oh, my God!" I exclaimed. "Here it is!"

The caption read: "IF DOGS COULD ONLY TALK." The story was as follows: "Last night Oslo police uncovered several female body parts in Kampen Park near the corner of Økernveien and Ensjoveien. The police were called to Kampen after a golden retriever and its owner discovered the woman's severed head. The dog had apparently been digging in the earth and delivered the decomposing head to its owner, who subsequently called the police to the scene. It is believed that the victim was sodomized, and that her neck was broken before her body was viciously hacked into pieces and buried separately. So far, no positive identification has been made of either victim or murderer. Police investigators speculate that the dog may have witnessed the murderer burying the victim's head. Anyone with information helpful to solving the case and identifying either victim or murderer, is urged to telephone the police."

When I reached the door of my flat, I was startled to look up from the newspaper and see Anne, Kåre's mother, standing at my door. She was out-of-breath and had a terrified look on her face. "Have you seen Kåre this afternoon?" she demanded anxiously.

"Why no, Anne", I replied.

"I thought he might be up here playing with the dog ...", she snapped nervously, and yet pleadingly.

"No, I've been out all afternoon," I replied. "You see, there was a body discovered in the part last night, and I was a witness sort of and, well, anyway, I had to go down to the police station to ..." I was rambling.

She cut me off: "Oh, God. I heard all about it! That's why I'm so worried about Kåre. I left him all alone in the backyard for an hour while I ran some errands. I don't do it often, but he was playing so contentedly by himself, and the sun was shining for the first time all week, and ... Well, it just seemed easier to leave him there for himself for a little while rather than dragging him around with me. I don't know where he could have gone!" She was most distraught and was speaking faster, and faster.

"Oh dear. Take it easy, Anne. I'm sure it's not anything serious. He's probably playing with some of his friends at their house," I said, trying to console and reassure her.

"No, he's not!" she cried hysterically. "I've looked everywhere! He's gone .. I <u>know it</u>. Something terrible has happened to him. I can feel it! Oh, please .. God, please help me!"

"Listen Anne .. just, just let me put these things in the apartment, and I'll help you look for him. I'm sure there's a simple and logical explanation. We'll find him .. you'll see. We'll find Kåre."

And so we began searching for little Kåre. With the help of the superintendent and his master keys, we went through every apartment in the building. Kåre was nowhere to be seen. We found the door to the attic surprisingly unlocked, but all looked to be in order. Finally, the superintendent noticed that the door from the backyard to the basement had been forced ajar. There, next to the boiler, he found the limp body of young Kåre — hanging from the ceiling by a dog collar and leash — with his eyeballs frozen wide open, and his nose gouged out.

"Don't let Anne in here!" he screamed to me. "It's the boy; he's .. dead."

Within the next fifteen minutes to one-half hour, the apartment building was swarming with police, reporters, and ambulance personnel — not for Kåre, it was too late for him; but for poor Anne, who was a last heavily sedated and carted off to the hospital. The superintendent and I told the police all that we knew, which was practically nothing, and I went back up to me flat to call Petter. It was now around 7:00 p.m., and there was no answer at Petter's apartment. He arrived, however, about 25 minutes later, having heard the news on the radio broadcast: "Kåre Holand, a nine-year-old deaf-mute, was found murdered in a basement today at Norderhovgata 73, at Kampen. No suspect has been named, but police believe the murder may be related to that of the butchered woman found buried in Kampen Park just 22 hours ago. Both victims had their noses gouged out of their faces in a similar fashion. Anyone — R-E-P-E-A-T —

<u>ANYONE</u> with information concerning either murder is urged to PLEASE NOTIFY THE POLICE IMMEDIATELY!"

"Turid!" cried Petter. "Are you alright?!! I just heard the news .." He was out-of-breath and very anxious. "I tried to call you but there was no answer, so I panicked and rushed right over," he explained.

"I don't understand what's happening, Petter," I whined. "I'm really scared!"

"Where have you been?" he demanded. "And why didn't you answer the telephone?"

"I've been down at Anne's apartment with the superintendent and the police. She's hysterical .. and they've taken her off to the hospital .."

Just then the doorbell rang. It was Lieutenant Tjæreborg. "Miss Alvdal," he said urgently. "I would like to have a word with you."

"Certainly, Lieutenant. Please come in," I replied.

He looked at Petter suspiciously.

"Lieutenant Tjæreborg," I blurted, "this is Petter Hansen — my agent and friend."

The lieutenant nodded at Petter, saying: "I see .. pleased to meet you. Miss Alvdal," he implored. "I've learned from some of your neighbors that Kåre often walked your dog?!!"

He was looking at me intensely again. I felt as if he were drilling a hole through my brain. "Why, yes Lieutenant. He doesn't, I mean, he didn't do so often. But I would occasionally pay him 10 crowns or so to take the dog out. It was more for the boy than for the dog, mind you. Jonny is very good with children, and Kåre has, uh .. had, som adjustment problems because of his disabili .."

Jonny walked over to me, hearing his name mentioned — wagging his tail and barking softly. The lieutenant gave him a pat on the head.

"His mother and I never saw any harm in it," I added.

"But why didn't you mention it before?" the lieutenant demanded. "I specifically asked you earlier about your routines with the dog, and ..."

"Now, wait a minute, Lieutenant," interjected Petter. "She's been under a terrific strain lately. You certainly can't expect her to rememb.."

"Petter — no!" I interrupted. "It's okay. Let me speak."

I realized that we were all still standing in the entrance hall. "Won't you have a seat Lieutenant?" We all sat down in the living room. "Do you think there is a connection between the two murders, Lieutenant Tjæreborg?" I asked.

"Frankly, yes," he responded. "Miss Alvdal — this is a very important question: had Kåre ever taken Jonny to the park by himself?"

"Yes," I replied. "The park is the only place nearby for dogs and children to run and play freely."

"And," the lieutenant continued, "had Kåre been outside with the dog over the past several weeks?"

"Yes," I said again. "Twice about three weeks or so ago. But not since. I think he had had a problem with some other kids, or was perhaps unhappy with Jonny the last time they were out, because he seemed a little distraught when they returned from their walk. He hasn't taken much interest in walking Jonny for a couple of weeks now .. Oh, my God!" I exclaimed, realizing what the lieutenant was getting at. "You think that the murderer saw Kåre and Jonny together?!! And that ..."

"And that the murderer killed little Kåre because he was a <u>witness</u>!" piped Petter.

"Precisely," confirmed the lieutenant.

"But Kåre couldn't speak! Why would he worry about a nine-year-old deaf-mute?" I asked quizzically.

"I never suggested that the murderer knew that Kåre couldn't speak, Miss Alvdal," corrected the lieutenant. "Only that if other persons from the neighborhood had seen Kåre with the dog — then perhaps the murderer had as well. Returning to the scene of the crime is more of a frequent occurrence than most people think. My own hunch is that the murderer actually resides in, or near Kampen ..."

"And," I chimed, "has been watching Kåre .. and .. Jonny .. for a very long time ...." My voice trailed off as I understood that danger lurked at my very doorstep. Petter sensed my fear and put his arm around me supportively.

"Not necessarily a long time," said the lieutenant.

"But perhaps a few weeks?" asked Petter, worriedly.

"Perhaps," replied the lieutenant. "But, let's not jump to too many conclusions yet. At least we have a little more to go on now. I'm confident that we'll catch him soon," reassured the lieutenant.

"Lieutenant Tjæreborg," asked Petter. "Is Turid in any danger?"

"I shouldn't think so," he replied. "She is not a witness to the crime; only to the remains. Stay calm and call me should any further unusual developments occur that may relate to the case in any way. I must be going now."

And with that, the lieutenant was off, and Petter and I spent the next several moments sitting on the sofa, speechless and worried.

The succeeding few days passed without incident. Petter insisted upon staying with me night and day. I didn't object too strongly at first, in light of the events that had recently come to pass. But, by the third early evening, we had begun to get on each other's nerves — or should I say, Petter got on mine.

I never could deal with feeling smothered ... by him or anyone else. As my sense of personal safety returned, so did my desire for independence. And so it happened that, on Tuesday, I picked a quarrel. It was pretty silly, actually. Petter had scheduled me for a modelling assignment the next morning, even though I had previously told him that I had planned to spend the day with my sister, who lived in Gjøvik. I went through the roof when he told me, and I screamed: "You are my AGENT, Petter. But you don't OWN ME! I distinctly told you that I'd planned to go to Gjøvik tomorrow, and you just totally disregarded ..."

"Oh, come on Turid," he broke in. "This is the kind of break we've been waiting for! It could easily develop into an entire advertising campain around you. Damn! You can see your sister anytime ...”

"I can see my sister, OR do anything ELSE I want, ANYTIME, Petter! Do you understand that? You've started taking over my entire life here." I was yelling irrationally now. My shoulders were high and tense, and I was trembling with rage.

Petter looked at me in astonishment, and asked: "What's really bothering you, Turid?" He touched my face sympathetically; and I pulled away.

Looking down at the carpet, rather than to meet his eyes, I said: "I'm sorry, Petter. I ... I just .." I slowly raised my eyes to engage his, and quietly said: "I need to be alone. Can you please .." This was difficult. "Can you please — leave?"

"I'll rearrange the job to another day if you want," he said. apologetically. "I didn't realize that it was so important for you to .."

"No," I said. "It's not just that, Petter. I need some time to think about things .. about you .. and me ..."

Petter held my hands again, and said with a forced cheerfulness: "I understand."

The next morning I was up early for the modelling assignment. I had walked Jonny around 5:00 a.m. — which was early even for him — so I knew he would be eager to go out again around 2:00 p.m. when I returned home. I guess that I sensed that something was awry as soon as I got inside the flat. Jonny didn't meet me at the door as he usually did. Then I noticed a trail of dark-red blood streaking the carpet from the entrance hall to the bedroom. I ran into the bedroom screaming, "Jonny .. <u>Jonny</u>!"

He had been stabbed several times in the neck and stomach. I began shrieking hysterically for «HELP.» Suddenly, the superintendent sprang from behind the closet door, where he had been hiding. He grabbed me from behind and firmly planted one hand over my mouth to prevent me from screaming, while restraining my frantic movements with his other hefty arm. I struggled, but to no avail. The superintendent then tied my hands together behind my back, and gagged my mouth with a piece of lingerie that he found lying on a bedside chair. It was then that I realized that we were not alone.

Reflected on the wall opposite from the closet was a third shadow, now moving toward us. I closed my eyes, crying a muffled "Oh, God. Please help me .. PLEASE!" When I opened them, I saw what appeared to be the twin of the superintendent, but horribly disfigured .. as if acid had eaten away parts of his face — his nose was missing entirely. In his hand was a bloody hunting knife. Terrified, my frantically convulsing body gave way to dizziness as the monstrous intruder slowly closed in on me.

And the last thing that I heard was the superintendent saying, "I'm terribly sorry, Miss Alvdal. But, you see .. he's .. he's family."

****

Adam Donaldson Powell is a professional writer, painter and international activist, working within the areas of art and culture, immigration politics, gay politics, health issues and assorted other sociopolitical issues etc. He was born in 1954 in Buffalo, New York, USA and is a naturalized citizen of Norway.

Adam Donaldson Powell's Publishing (and stage performance) Credits:

The Prudent Cognoscente:

- Explorers: A Collection of Contemporary Literature, ISBN 8182530180, 2004, India.

Daedalus: Elegy:

- Taj Mahal Review: An International Journal Devoted to Arts, Literature, Poetry and Culture, ISSN 0972-6004, 2004, India.

The Scalding:

- Weirdbook issue #28, 1993, USA.

Nighthawk:

- Weirdbook Encores #12, 1992, USA.
- Being Magazine, April 1990, ISSN 0898-4034, USA.

Le Gibet:

- Weirdbook 27, Spring 1992, ISBN 8755-7452, USA.
- Poetry Break Journal, July/August 1989, ISSN 0985-7233, USA.

Birth of the Minotaur:

- Amanita Brandy, issue #3, 1992, USA.
- Being Magazine, February 1990, ISSN 0898-4034, USA.

Forever Young:

- Amanita Brandy, issue #4, 1999, USA.
- Poetry Break Journal, December 1989, ISSN 085-7233, USA.

Retrospective:

- Dream International Quarterly, 1989 nr. 11, ISBN 0912-3075, Australia and USA.

Psyche and Phantasy:

- Being Magazine, Vol. 3 nr. 5, 1991, ISSN 0898-4034, USA.

Nocturnal Journey:

- Being Magazine, Vol. 3 nr. 5, 1991, ISSN 0898-4034, USA.

Green:

- Poetry Break Journal, Sept./Oct. 1991, ISSN 0895-7233, USA.
- A Galaxy of Verse, Fall 1990, USA.

Le Moment:

- Poetry Break Journal, Sept./Oct. 1991, ISSN 0895-7233, USA.

Cloudburst:

- Poetry Break Journal, May/June 1991, ISSN 0895-7233, USA.
- A Galaxy of Verse, Spring/Summer 1990, USA.

Razor Roulette:

- A Galaxy of Verse, Spring/Summer 1990, USA.

Dog Days:

- A Galaxy of Verse, Fall 1990, USA.

The Death of Poetry:

- A Galaxy of Verse, Fall 1988, USA.

While We Wait:

- A Galaxy of Verse, Fall 1988, USA.

Deja Vu:

- A Galaxy of Verse, Spring 1989, USA.

Rage of Daedalus:

- Weirdbook issue #29, 1995, USA.
- Being Magazine, June 1990, ISSN 0898-4034, USA.

The Dissident Android:

- Poetry Break Journal, May/June 1989, ISSN 085-7233, USA.

Writer's Blues:

- Poetry Break Journal, May/June 1989, ISSN 085-7233, USA.

Peer Group Heroes:

- Being Magazine, Vol. 4 nr. 1, 1992, ISSN 0898-4034, USA.

Rhythm and Tears:

- Being Magazine, August 1990, ISSN 0898-4034, USA.
- Poetry Break Journal, Sept./Oct. 1990, ISSN 085-7233, USA.

Drag Queen, Stud and Celluloid Sex Magic:

- First Hand Magazine, 1988-1990, USA.

Notes of a Madman, (hardback collection of poetry containing following titles: Notes of a Madman, Hyacinth, Truth is a Whore, The Zen of Sorcery, Spleen, The Chalice, The Abortion, Absurdities of Perception, Mirror of Darkness, Rite of Passage, Anno Humanae Salutis, Agitations of the Heart, Hieros Gamos, Void of Course, The Archetypal Kouros, IAO, The Eye of the Triangle and The Coming), Winston-Derek Publishers, Inc., 1987, ISBN 1-55523-054-7, USA (now out-of-print).

Daedalus: an ancient epic for modern man:

- performed on stage in Oslo, Norway by Blått Paradis Dance Theater Company, 1987-88 at:
- Black Box Theater, Edvard Munch Museum, etc.

Various works read at Volapuk (Oslo) in 2000 and 2001.

Arcana and other archetypes, (hardback collection of poetry), AIM Chapbooks ANS, 2001, Norway.